Granny Nancy's Cook Book

Granny Nancy's Cook Book

Nancy Douglass

AuthorHouse™
1663 Liberty Drive
Bloomington, IN 47403
www.authorhouse.com
Phone: 1-800-839-8640

Published by AuthorHouse 10/18/2012

ISBN: 978-1-4772-8069-0 (sc)
ISBN: 978-1-4772-8068-3 (e)

Library of Congress Control Number: 2012919479

Introduction

This recipe book is sooo good!
People that don't even cook LOVE to read it!

In this book I am introducing many of my personal thoughts that I shall refer to as opinion recipes. Not everything that I say will fit everybody, I wrote info as I see it although you have the option as a reader to either use it or loose it. LOL

It's up to the reader to make choices, my book is not telling you what to do. I just tend to suggest a lot. Capishe? I hope all my opinion recipes are helpful and inspiring. I just want to help everyone see things clearly hopefully before you are in a situation that you prefer not to be.

Now, as far as the food recipes, you will find recipes in this book that are my very own creations and recipes that have been shared with me sometimes not knowing where they originated. And there are those recipes that have been passed down in my family...some for many generations.

Nancy Douglass

In Memory of.....

First and foremost, I would like to give honor to God whom I believe to be my creator.

I want to thank God for his greatness and the gift of my parents Paul & Lillian La Bahn. They are both on their way to be with God but they both have left me a lifetime of memories. So I want to dedicate this book to them and the many loves of my life who have gone on. Thank you for the love I will never forget!

I dedicate this book to my Mom and Dad.
Lillian and Paul La Bahn
May they Rest in Peace.

Special Thanks

To Lionel,

My Husband, My Lover, My Partner, My Very Bestest Friend, My Road Dog, My Precious Heart. I have the utmost respect, gratitude, and admiration for the help you have so freely given to me.

My husband, "Lionel Douglass", is a large force in the makings of Granny Nancy and all my endeavors. He is my unsung Hero. Supportive, loving, and so so smart. He always comes to the table with wonderful ideas, commitment, and enthusiasm. He sees, as always, the big picture, and is a great visionary. He has encouraged me to just keep plugging along writing my little heart out while he makes other things continue to happen. Through God and you I have been given the opportunity to live a remarkable life. I love you with all my heart Lionel.

Nancy

Mentions

My Daughter's, Mikhail and Jevon, my son-in-law Ron, my Grandchildren; Dominique (Niko), Diego, Dillon, Shay & RJ

Who have all contributed tremendously in growing my wisdom. God has truly Blessed me with the best family anyone could ask for.

A shout out to more family & friends whom I Love dearly and who loved my cooking.... Jesus, Aunt Carol, Uncle Eddie & Fam, Peggy, Jeff, Paul, Mary, Craig, Donna, Van, Del, Lisa, Jason LaBahn, Myranda, Jaydyn, Lindsay, Gavin, Evan, Nicole, Connor, Ross, Nikki & Aaron, Kelsey, Kyle, Lauren, Jason Coleman & Justin Jr., Chucky Cymone, Tanya, Lo, Justin, Chris Gibson & Boys, The Martinez's, The Moyer's, Rosa, The Love's, Magda & Fam, Gilbert & Dee, Umberto Archer, Jen & Jetaime Jackson, Sheila & Fam, Jacqueline, Michelle, Taylor T., Vinnie & Fam, Jody & Fam, Suzi, Thomas Gavin, Mahvash, Kisha, Doug Batchelor & Fam, Roxanne Cuba, Jesse Lynnwood, Chiara, Colleen, Chrissy, Tina & Ray, Annette Shultz, Judy Johnson & Fam. Zakiya & Stacey, Thea, Aliyah and Gregory, Glenda & Fam, Dr. J, Skip & Lottie & Fam, Sam & Carm Mercurio, Tippie, JoAnne, and a few of my husband's old buddies, Deputy, Kevin, Alpha, Casper, Cooley and many more....................and last but not least "Ralph" and all his children.

Join me as I share some of my thoughts and favorite quotes. Some of these things I think and then other things I just suggest that you may want to think about. Many I simply learned from life experience. If you read my book I can save you a lot of trouble in life regarding many situations as I tend to just cut to the chase.
Perhaps the way I say it would be deemed as a no brainer?

I have so many various kinds of recipes, there is no other book in the world that is the same as this one. Check out the many different kinds of recipes:

Various Recipes on ....
MEAL RECIPES
LOVE RECIPES
DATING RECIPES
CHILDREN RECIPES
WISDOM RECIPES
HEALTH and healthy STUFF RECIPES
MOTIVATION RECIPES
SMART SHOPPING.............and more.......

JUST A SAMPLE OF ONE OF MY MANY "THOUGHT RECIPES" TO BE FOUND IN THIS BOOK:

RECIPE FOR WISDOM

THE ROAD TO WISDOM IS LONG BUT THERE IS A SHORTCUT: LISTEN TO YOUR MOM (or me, Granny).
Just saying. So............ READ THIS BOOK AND try it my way. LOL

GRANNY NANCY

THE PURPOSE OF THE MEAL

The purpose of a meal is to satisfy hunger and to give pleasure. Remember, after hunger is satisfied, more food is a hindrance to health. After the appetite has been stimulated by a variety of foods, to stimulate it further simply jades it. Capishe?

At one time it was the custom to serve long and elaborate dinners having many courses. Gradually the realization has grown that elaborate meals are not justified from any point of view, social, physiological or economic, and that even the most formal meal must follow the rules of health.

There you have it, I heard and now I have said it.

ENJOY THE RECIPES.........

Table of Contents

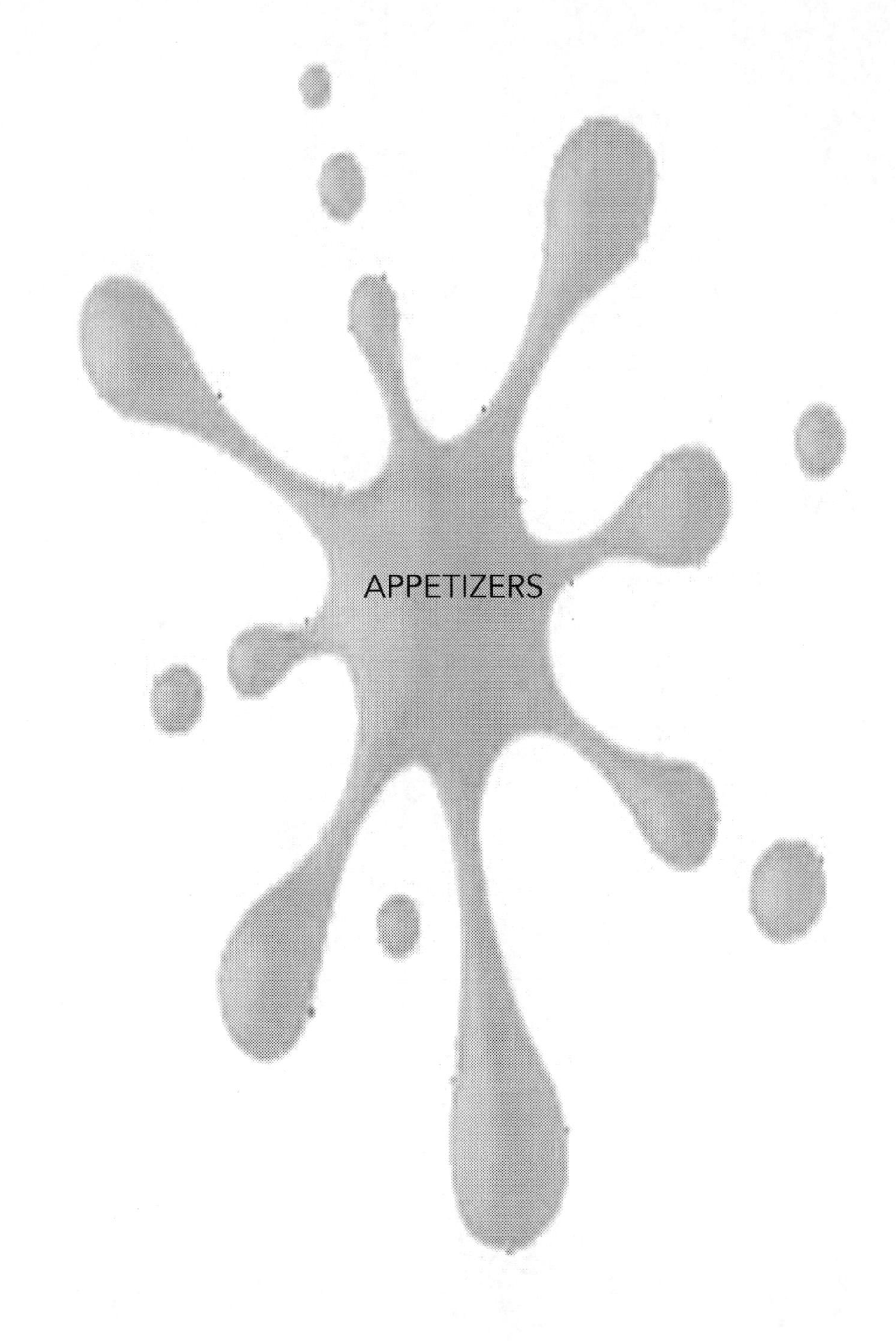

APPETIZERS

About APPETIZERS

Ok, so here's the deal:

The "appetizer" initially was an introduction to the meal. Typically because of their savory qualities. Sometimes they are referred to as "Hors d'oeuvres. Actually, the appetizer from my point of view has become a separate course by itself and even sometimes an entire meal because they can be very filling. Many people often begin their dinner out with a salad or an appetizer. (sometimes I just eat an Appetizer for my whole meal)

A good idea when serving Appetizers at home is to always serve in small portions because the purpose of this course is to "whet" but not to satisfy the appetite.

If you want to get fancy with it and give guest the opportunity to choose their own appetizer, you can have a number of portions of various kinds arranged on a tray or platter, which you can have passed to each guest. Each portion should be arranged so that it may be lifted from the tray by the guest and transferred to a small plate without trouble. Wasn't that said so eloquently? LOL

Or of course you can have them sitting out buffet style as well. The following pages will have a couple of ideas for appetizers..........

Just a few. Smile.

CHIPS and FRESH TOMATO SALSA

1 cup peeled, seeded, chopped Tomatoes or fresh Tomatillos*
¼ cup thinly sliced green Onions (green & white part)
2 tablespoons finely chopped green Pepper (use red peppers if using Tomatillos)
1 Jalapeño Pepper, seeded and minced (pop in micro wave for 30 seconds)
1 ½ tablespoons Lime juice (I prefer fresh Lime)
1 teaspoon Salt
½ teaspoon freshly ground black Pepper
1 teaspoon Olive Oil or Garlic oil
2 tablespoons Cilantro

*Tomatillos" - if you cannot find them in your grocery store then you will find them in Spanish grocery stores or specialty supermarket produce sections. (Don't use canned Tomatillos as they are too watery and mushy)

Stir tomato, green onions, jalapeno peppers, lime juice, salt, pepper oil and cilantro together. Let sit for 10 minutes before serving at room temperature.

Taste and add more seasonings if you choose.

You may want to double this recipe as this is a rather small amount.

ENJOY!

Interesting Tip from Granny Nancy

Just a thought for you to think about for starters:
100 percent whole grain carbs can make you produce more of the feel good chemical serotonin, while fat and protein reduce it. Think about that. Why not do everything to feel as good as we can. Write this down! LOL

Dr. J's Grilled Scallop Appetizer
Okay, ok.... this is not a Dr. J's original
He got it from somewhere and it is Great!
Except for the tomatoes, he added that HIMSELF for some visual interest.
So............ Capishe?

Things you'll need:

- 20 large sea Scallops
- Olive oil
- Salt
- Freshly ground black Pepper
- 20 Round Tortilla Chips
- Avocado Puree, recipe follows
- Jalapeño Pesto, recipe follows
- Cilantro leaves, for garnish

Directions

Heat grill to high. Brush scallops on both sides with the oil and season with salt and pepper. Grill the scallops until golden brown and slightly charred and just cooked through, 2 to 3 minutes per side.

Spread about a tablespoon of avocado puree over each chip. Top the puree with a scallop

Jalapeno pesto. Garnish with cilantro leaves.

Avocado Puree:

FoR: DR J'S Grilled Scallop Appetizer

- 1 ripe Avocado, peeled, pitted, chopped
- 2 tablespoons chopped red Onion
- 2 Limes, juiced
- 2 tablespoons Olive Oil
- 1/4 cup chopped fresh Cilantro leaves
- Salt
- Freshly ground black Pepper

Combine all ingredients in a food processor and process until combined, but still chunky. Puree until smooth, if desired. OR, heck just chopped up real small.

Dr. J's Grilled Scallop Appetizer

Jalapeño Pesto:

- 1 1/2 cups Cilantro leaves
- 4 Jalapenos, grilled and chopped. Remove seeds if you don't want it real HOT!
- 1 clove Garlic, chopped
- Salt
- Freshly ground black Pepper
- 1/2 cup extra-virgin Olive oil

Combine cilantro, jalapeno, garlic, salt and pepper in a food processor and process until coarsely chopped. With the motor running, slowly add the oil and process until emulsified. Scrape into a bowl. OR AGAIN......JUST CHOP ALL REAL SMALL.

ENJOY!

RECIPES FOR WOMEN
MY LITTLE RECIPES LOL LOL

a word on high heels..........
great for a visual slimming effect - every woman must have a sexy pair of pumps. (even if you only wear them a couple of moments, always carry a matching pair of flats, they have little ones that fit in your purse) Hint; sometimes you only need to wear them for your initial entrance. Think about it. Hmmm.............

take care of your hands..........
You touch people with them, talk with them, serve food with them. Don't betray your hands, it's not cute.

Use good hair products..........don't believe for 1 minute cheap products are just as good! K'MON! REALLY?
Think about it..........Hair companies spend a lot of money on research and development. So customized hair products actually work. If you are thinking you can't squeeze that extra couple of dollars, put it in perspective. Most luxury brands of shampoo and conditioners are higher concentrated which means a nickel size amount goes a lot further than less expensive brands consequently lasting just as long or longer. You do the math.

Touch up your hair color right away........ don't let the gray peek through. (it is tacky looking) If times are tuff - cut back on the starbucks. Or better yet don't die your hair at all, let it grow all the way out and be done with it. Just do one or the other. Capishe?

Use a water purifier in your shower......................
it will do wonders for your hair.

on Large heavy purses......... if you can't walk through a crowded area with your purse on your shoulder without bumping everybody......maybe it is time to take inventory. Also, remember anything too big and heavy will take it's toll on our posture. We all know the bigger the bag the more we put in it and the bigger the strap indentation on our shoulder which will be there forever. This is Not attractive. Smile because you know it. I know it cause I have that indentation on my shoulder. Just sayin...... LOL

RECIPE TO DEAL WITH PEOPLE WHO PUSH YOUR BUTTONS

Think about this..........

Trigger points? We all have things we are extra sensitive about, right? Well, sometimes certain people can push those buttons? Right? If you see it getting ready to happen, go the other way. (HINT: look at your cell phone suddenly and say; OMG I forgot, I have to go and scurry on off)....no explanations, it works every time) And I say no explanations because there is no sense in lying! Just; I have got to go", that's it. You must remember, your time is precious so don't waste it on unimportant things such as someone attempting to create drama - or their intent to be mean to you.

This is a great recipe to practice.......... Just get out of dodge! Simple enough? Capishe? Don't stick around for drama! If you stick around then you must like it? You choose. LOL

GUACAMOLE, my way.

4 Avocados
1 10 ounce can Rotele
½ cup chopped Green Onions (diced)
3 Tomatoes (diced)

DON'T FORGET THE CHIPS!

OR.............here's another little Guacamole recipe..........

Avocado
chopped Onions
chopped, seeded Jalapeño chile
chopped Cilantro
chopped Tomato
Salt

AGAIN, DON'T FORGET THE CHIPS!
See next Chip recipe.

ENJOY!

HOMEMADE TORTILLA CHIPS
TO GO WITH THE "GUACAMOLE"

Things you'll need:

- Vegetable Oil
- 1 package Corn Tortilla's
- Sea Salt or Salt (just a note: Sea Salt does not contain iodine)
- Tongs and a Fork (you will need these, so have them out and ready. You don't want to fumble for them once your cooking and oil is heated.
- A platter of some sort covered with paper towels to lay the cooked tortilla on to allow excess oil to drain
-

Open Tortilla's.
Lay on bread board or plate or something and cut in half and then in half again. Now you have tortilla shaped chips. (Or sometimes I just leave the tortilla whole and fry it and let everyone take a big phat glob of Guacamole and spread it across the tortilla and chow down). LOL
Pour some vegetable oil in a frying pan.
Turn burner onto medium. (Do not leave unattended as cooking oil heats up rather quickly).
Once the vegetable oil is heated, lay the tortilla in the pan and it will automatically submerse under the cooking oil. Have your tongs in your hand and let cook on each side for a about a minute. (depends if you like extra crispy or not, you decide).

ENJOY!

Sweetheart Meatballs
This can be an easy appetizer!
Soooo Sweeeet!
for Lionel my sweet biscuit

You can use this sauce for Turkey meatballs too.!

Things you'll need:

1 -14 oz can Jellied Cranberry sauce
¾ cup grape Jelly

Combine both ingredients in a saucepan.
Cook over medium-low heat, stirring until smooth.
Add to meatballs.
Cover and cook for 15 minutes or until meatballs are heated through, stirring occasionally.

-or-

Do the slower cooker preparation:

Place meatballs in a slow cooker. (crock pot)
Combine sauces and pour over meatballs.
Cover and cook 4 hours on HIGH.

After being cooked:

Arrange on a Platter of some sort and stick a toothpick (a cute toothpick) in each one and serve.

ENJOY!

PRACTICE RECIPE OF IMPORTANCE

Something to Practice..........

Don't always say EXACTLY what is on your mind.....often it needs to be softened.

(Think for awhile first, then speak)

This is not easy, but you will have less regrets.

Recipe for Grocery Shopping

And

A word or two on over eating......

Plan, Plan, Plan! Buy the right foods at the store and it will be easier to eat "right" when you are at home. (because those will be your only choices, right? Do ya GET IT? Smile) Also, shop along the walls in the grocery store - it's that simple. There you will have your fish, poultry, veggies, fruits and dairy. Steer away from going up and down the isles, it's basically boxes and cans full of chemicals. Capishe?

Just another Granny Nancy Tip. Love ya!

Also.........remember as I say often; if it (the food) has spent more time in the factory than in the ground, it is probably junk, right?

SEVEN LAYER DIP

I know......EVERYBODY KNOWS THIS ONE.
I'm just reminding you of a good idea.

1 16 ounce can refried Beans
1 1.25 ounce package Taco seasoning mix
8 ounce Sour Cream
8 ounce Guacamole (homemade is best)
2 cups Mexican Four Cheese blend
1 cup Salsa (I like homemade)
1 cup diced green Chiles
1/3 cup sliced green Onions
A bag of Tortilla chips

Combine beans and taco seasoning mix in a small bowl.
Spread over bottom of 8-inch square baking dish.
Layer sour cream, guacamole, 1 cup of cheese, salsa, chiles and green onions.
Top with rest of the cheese and serve with tortilla chips

ENJOY!

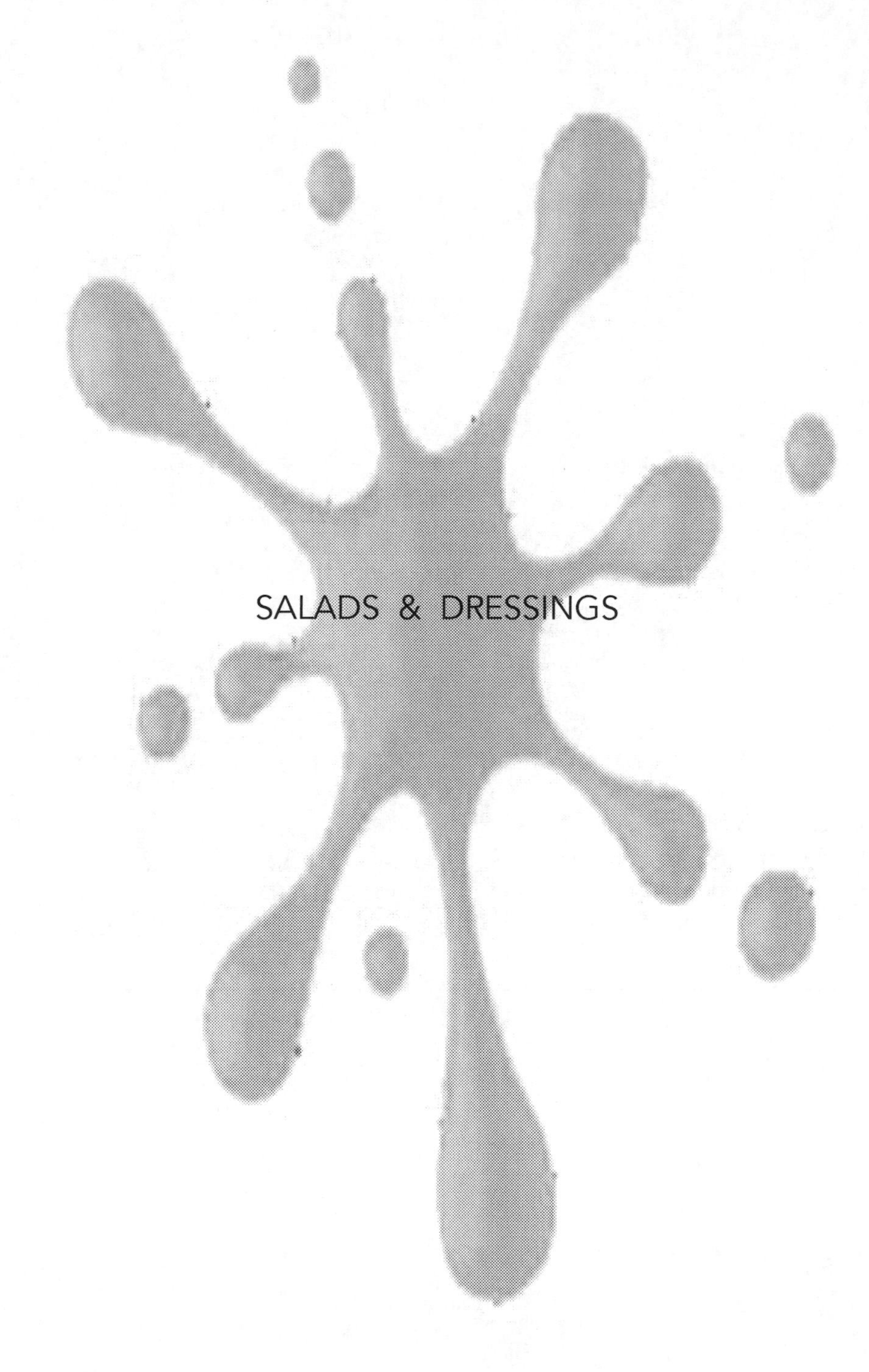

SALADS & DRESSINGS

ABOUT Salads

Ok, a lot of people in this day and age deem "Salad" sometimes as a dietary meal. Although, sometimes we load up our salads with so much stuff that it is no longer low calorie nor a diet dish. Know what I'm saying? (Something to think about)

Anyway.....food historians say the Romans ate mixed greens and dressing, and the Babylonians were known to have dressed greens with oil and vinegar two thousand years ago, believe it or not. Just a little trivia for you!

The United States popularized salads in the late 19th century and then other regions of the world adopted them in the second half of the 20th century. So they basically copy catt-ed us. LOL

Anyway, back to the point. Salad is any of a wide variety of dishes including; vegetable salads, salads of pasta, legumes, eggs, or grains; now we have salads that incorporate meat, poultry, seafood and fruit. Crazy!

Well, here's the deal, I don't have all those salad recipes in this book. But! One of the reasons I wrote this book is not only to give recipes but also to give "Ideas" for recipes - or should I just say ideas of what to fix, eat, prepare or serve? You understand if you cook a lot, you sometimes just can't think of what to cook. But if you see something, read something or hear something then you can just run with it. Capishe?

So moving forward I have provided some salad recipes and then below I have named just a few ideas you can run with. Sometimes if we just have a basic starting point we can google that item along with the word recipe and come up with a new dish to cook. Right? Or for that matter we can just create it.

So check it out: (you could use this for your grocery list and just stay healthy with it, know what I'm saying?

Common vegetables used in salads include cucumber, peppers, tomatoes, mushrooms, onions, spring onions, red onions, avocado, carrots, celery and radishes. Other ingredients, such as olives, hard boiled egg, artichoke hearts, hearts of palm, roasted red bell peppers, green beans, croutons, cheeses.

Wow, that will give anybody a good start. Don't let me get started on "Lettuce"; there are so many kinds. Just choose the one you like. I like Romaine because it doesn't seem to wilt *as fast as the others. Just a note you may want to make. That is just my own opinion. Smile.*

Now here is one the many suggestions, I mentioned, so please use these when you need or want to come up with something different for a salad, ok? It will be things like this that help you out when you just can't think of what to fix , or when nothing sounds good or when your'e just plain tired of the same ole stuff. Just sayin..................

Bean Salad
Broccoli Salad
Chef Salad
Chicken Salad
Chinese Chicken Salad
Coleslaw Salad
Crab Louie Salad
Egg Salad
Fruit Salad
Pasta Salad
Potato Salad
Ham Salad
Seven Layer Salad
Taco Salad
Tuna Salad
Waldorf Salad

Here some ideas for Salad Dressings that may come in handy too:

Italian Dressing
Blue Cheese Dressing
Caesar Dressing
Extra Virgin Olive Oil Dressing (with a twist of lemon of course)
French Dressing
Honey Dijon Dressing
Hummus Dressing
Louis Dressing
Ranch Dressing
Rice Vinegar Dressing
Russian Dressing
Thousand Island Dressing
Vinaigrette Dressing

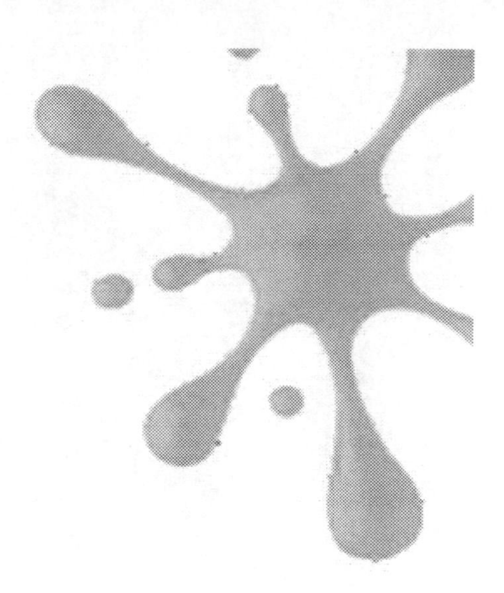

HAVE FUN WITH THIS LITTLE DRESSING IDEA:

IT WILL BE KIND OF LIKE A VINAIGRETTE DRESSING..................

INGREDIENTS:

Fresh Tomatoes
Garlic (about 1 clove)
Red Wine Vinegar
Fruity Extra Virgin Olive Oil
Black Pepper
Sea Salt
Red Bell Pepper (put on flame of gas stove and burn, then remove inside

Put all in blender and just blend, blend, blend

You tweek the recipe how you see fit.

ENJOY!

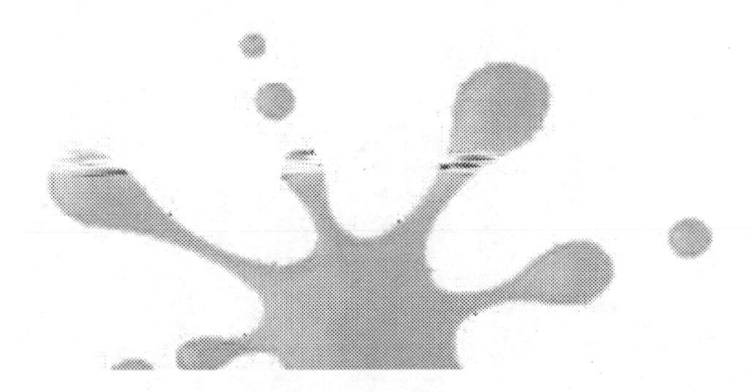

Recipe from Life experience

Don't suffer for something you once said because you spoke too soon....

A great recipe to follow:

Just imagine that everything you say is going to be seen on the front page of every newspaper or heard on the 6:00 news. You'll think twice about saying it, right? Trust me having this thought before you speak, write or email anything will save you lots of grief in your lifetime. No regrets! Know what I'm saying? Especially keep this in mind if you are emotionally upset, hurt or angry. Do not respond when emotional, period.

Take it a step further and use my

"Delay to avoid Regret Recipe"

DELAY/REGRET RECIPE AS FOLLOWS:

Delay responding to anything upsetting for 48 hours!!

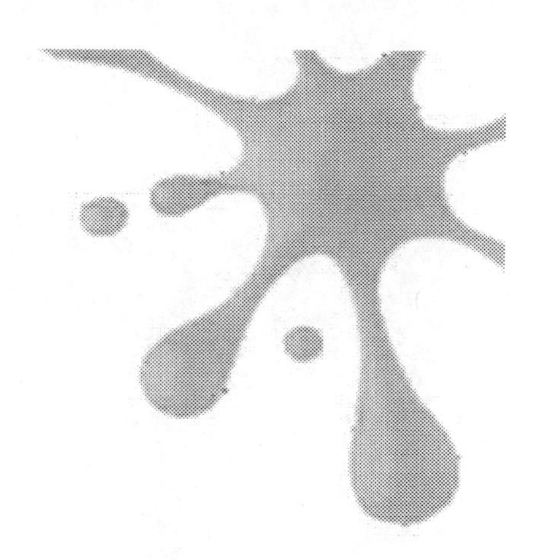

SPINACH SALAD

Ingredients:

4 slices Canadian bacon (your choice as you can substitute with Turkey bacon)
3 Tablespoons extra-virgin Olive Oil
2 Tablespoons Balsamic Vinegar
½ Teaspoon Dijon Mustard
Salt & freshly ground Pepper to taste
8 ounces baby Spinach leaves (about 8 cups lightly packed)
2 cups cherry or grape tomatoes, cut in half
4 hard-boiled eggs, peeled and chopped
½ cup chopped fresh flat-leaf parsley

Cook your bacon in a skillet until golden brown.
Remove from the skillet and cut into small pieces. Set aside.

In a bowl, whisk together the oil, vinegar and mustard. Season with salt and pepper.

Place the Spinach in a large serving bowl. Add the dressing and toss to coat evenly. Top with the Tomatoes, Eggs, Bacon and Parsley.

Serve and **ENJOY!**

Avo-Berry Salad

Things you'll need:

Fresh Blueberries (about 2 cups or to your liking)
Avocado (2 cups, peeled and cut in squares)
2 tomatoes (diced)

Dressing Ingredients:

1/2 cup Olive oil
3 tablespoon Lemon Juice
2 Teaspoon Honey
Salt & Pepper

Ok, let's begin........this is what you will need:

Medium sized glass bowl.

Wash tomatoes and dice rather small and put in medium size glass bowl.

Wash Avocado, cut in half, slice squares while avocado is inside the skin, then scoop out with a spoon into glass dish.

Rinse fresh Blueberries and drain, add to glass dish with Avocado tomatoes.

Dressing Instructions

Combine all dressing ingredients in some type of container where you will be able to shake really good such as a glass jar.

ENJOY!

RECIPE TO KNOW WHAT NOT TO EAT

Again, I can't stress it enough.................................Be smart........choose unrefined and unprocessed foods over foods that have spent more time in a factory than in the earth.
If it's in a box....forget about it. LOL

Hmmm, think about that!

MAKES SENSE, HUH?

Baja Chicken Pasta

Hey everyone, you are going to love this dish! It will turn out great! You can actually have it hot or cold. Check it out!

This recipe seems long but it is not. It's just that I have a lot to say as I want you to be information empowered. Smile. So......don't be put off by the length of the recipe. Capishe?

Things you'll need:

Your choice of amounts: (go ahead and add lots of your favorite ingredient – it's a free country, LOL)

This can be a warm or cold dish – your choice.........

1 bag Multi colored Spiral Pasta
4 to 6 Chicken Breast (cut in cubes)
1 big Bell Pepper
1 can black Olives
½ cup sun-dried Tomatoes
1 bunch Cilantro
1 Onion (red)
1 tablespoon Lemon -or- Lemon juice
2 dashes lemon Pepper
2 dashes Mrs. Dash seasoning
Olive oil
Apple Cider Vinegar
½ teaspoon Salt
½ teaspoon Pepper
3 dashes Tony Chachere's Creole Seasoning (optional, depends if you like spicy or not).

Cut all the fat off the chicken, it's nasty!
Wash and rinse chicken.
Salt and Pepper Chicken breast lightly.
If you like, you can lightly spray baking pan with Pam.
Lay chicken in baking pan (do not arrange chicken pieces too close together, at least an inch apart)..
Cook at 425 degrees for about 20 minutes,

SEE NEXT PAGE...

After 20 minutes, cut through thickest part of chicken and confirm there are no pink juices left. If so, put chicken back in oven for about 3 minutes – at this point time is crucial! Just a couple minutes too much and you will have DRY nasty chicken. So listen up. LOL

Once chicken is cooked, take out and set aside to cool off.

Now.........wash everything you used to prepare chicken. Rinse with hot/warm soapy water. (like the colander, cutting board, knife etc)

Now, get the comet and scrub the sink and rinse the sink really good) This is to avoid contamination.

While chicken is cooking, boil water for Pasta.
Cook pasta for about 8 to 10 minutes. (DO NOT OVERCOOK)
See directions on package of pasta if need be.
Drain Pasta and cool off.

Rinse bell peppers, slice in half and remove seeds then slice in thick strips.
Open black olives and drain juice.
Cut sun-dried tomatoes up.
Rinse cilantro really good and dry on paper towel. (look carefully as sometimes there is mud on the leaves.
Chop cilantro.
Peel red onion and slice any way you like. (in strips or squares)

Now, your chicken and your pasta should be cooled off.

With a sharp knife, cut your chicken in cubes.

Into a large glass bowl add the chicken and pasta.
Toss in bell peppers. Black olives, sun-dried tomatoes, cilantro, onion, 2 dashes lemon pepper, 1 to 2 dashes Italian seasoning, 3 dashes Tony Chachere's Seasoning.

Combine the following ingredients to make the dressing in a jar of some sort as you will need to shake it up really really good.

SEE NEXT PAGE...

Baja Chicken Recipe Dressing

Things you'll need:

½ cup olive oil (or any flavored olive oil of your choice)
¼ tablespoon apple cider vinegar (or flavored balsamic vinegar of your choice)
1 tablespoon lemon juice
½ teaspoon black pepper
½ teaspoon salt

After mixing together, shake really good and immediately add to bowl of pasta and chicken and other ingredients and toss all together.

No need to use all the dressing you have made, in fact use just a little to give flavor.

Less is better (~_~)

ENJOY!

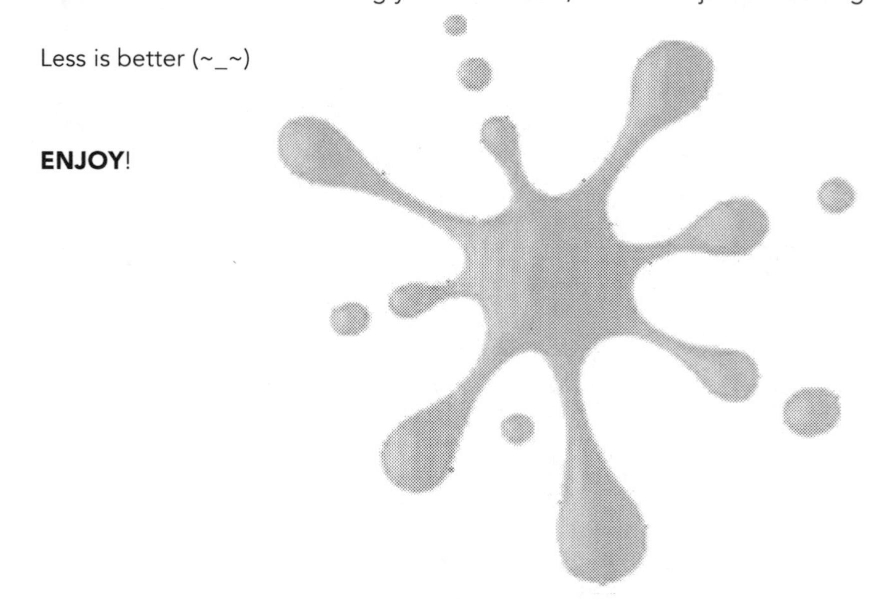

Here is another strong opinion of mine, I have a feeling there are many others who may agree with me on this next one..........

A WORD ON:
GIFT GIVING

Everyone is asking for cash these days...
just give us money, they say $$$ .... but geez!

The substitution of money in exchange for a gift you have chosen for that particular person is practical but it strips the custom of thoughtfulness and charm.
Don't you agree?

Or how about I cut to the chase......

(besides that, REALLY? how about the person that doesn't have that much to spend that week? Now you strip them of trying to get something inexpensive but thoughtful, because now the requester of the gift wants to put the dollar amount on BLAST, should I say... they kind of back you into a corner because of their Greed?!
Just sayin..........

How about the old:
Love the gift you get and be
"Grateful"
What happened to that?

Recipe to understand not to ask others for YOUR next dream?

Oh , and just a word to the wise for those of you out there that send notes, or even cleverly suggest to others that you prefer a monetary donation over a gift? We all get it. No matter how you proclaim it, here is the bottom line: "You are scheming to ask others to pay for your honeymoon, vacation, your current dream or what ever it is." Well, it may come as a shock to you but your weddings, birthdays, Christmas etc etc should not carry admission fees. Geez? How Rude is that? There is no polite way to ask people, guest, family or just others in general to pretend to not know that you want them to finance your wants, your dreams etc.

(Graduations not included, it is acceptable to help young adults going for an education)

CHINESE CHICKEN SALAD
(yields about 8 servings)

This is an entire meal!

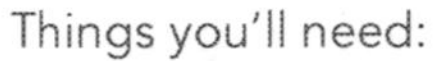

Things you'll need:

4 to 6 Skinless Chicken Breast
2 bags pre -cut Cole Slaw mix (or shredded cabbage)
2 packages Top Ramen (Oriental Flavor) Set seasoning packet aside for dressing)
1 package sliced Almonds
1 Bunch Green Onions
1 package Sesame Seeds
Optional: 2 small cans Mandarin Orange sections

- Wash chicken, drain. NO need to season at all.
- Bake on 425 degrees for 20 minutes on top rack. After 20 minutes.... check chicken by cutting into thickest part of chicken and make sure juice is clear. Take out and set out to cool off.
- While chicken is baking, roast sesame seeds and almonds in oven for about 5 minutes and set aside to cool off. (this is optional you can add to salad just as they are if you like)
- Pour bag of shredded cabbage (coleslaw mix) into large glass bowl, add chopped green onions, almonds, and sesame seeds
- Once chicken is cooled off, cut into bit size pieces and add to the rest of the salad.
- Take top ramen and break up while still in packaging then open package and set seasoning packets aside. Take dry broken up top ramen and sprinkle in salad bowl.
- Do not add mandarin orange sections till just before serving to prevent the rest of the ingredients from getting soggy.

SEE INSTRUCTIONS TO MAKE DRESSING ON NEXT PAGE..............................

OPTIONAL:

You can brown the Almonds and Sesame seeds in olive oil if you like or continue to follow instructions and roast them. (or don't do nothing at all and just sprinkle them into the salad as you mix everything together. I have done it all different ways and it is great!

CHINESE CHICKEN SALAD DRESSING

2 cups vegetable oil
½ cup Rice Vinegar (Plain flavor – no spices)
½ cup Sugar
½ cup juice from the Mandarin Oranges
2 packages seasoning mix from Top Ramen
½ teaspoon Salt
½ teaspoon Pepper

INSTRUCTIONS FOR DRESSING

- in container mix the Rice Vinegar, Sugar, Salt, Pepper and Seasoning mix packets from Top Ramen. (I usually use a glass jar) You must make sure the lid closes tightly because you must shake vigorously as ingredients are inclined to separate.

Shake, Shake and Shake, then add the Vegetable oil and Mandarin Orange juice and SHAKE Vigorously. SET ASIDE FOR SALAD.

Serve in salad bowl and pour dressing on individually so that salad will not become soggy! You must shake dressing just before pouring as it will separate in seconds.

ENJOY!

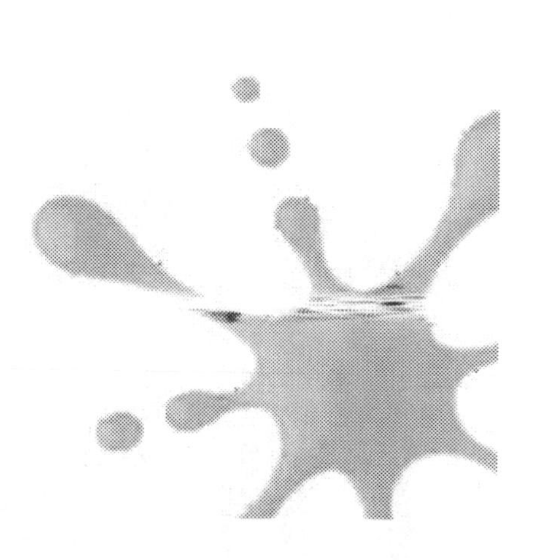

RECIPE FOR A GREAT THOUGHT ON CHILDREN & PARENTS

The job of any parent is to raise a child who ultimately will acquire a healthy, separate self. Begin their own life and also embrace the Fifth Commandment, Honor thy Father and Mother.

Appreciate when your parent(s) finally have a life of their own and just as importantly be grateful that they don't try to live your life for you. As well as the greatest love a parent can offer a child is the encouragement for their child to get a life and go ahead and live it and don't worry about us parents.

SOMEONE SAID THAT!

This is especially for grown children who don't think to consider their parents happiness what ever their situation may be....

COLESLAW

Ingredients:

4 cups Cabbage (shredded)
½ cup green Bell pepper (chopped)
½ cup green Onions (diced)
About ¼ cup Mayo (or add as you like)
¼ cup heavy Whipping Cream
1 tsp. sugar
1 tsp. Apple Cider Vinegar
¼ tsp. Salt

You can purchase cabbage pre-shredded by buying the bag that says coleslaw.

Put cabbage/coleslaw in glass bowl.

Wash green bell pepper and chop into squares add to glass bowl.

Peel onion and dice in little squares and add to bowl.

Put ¼ cup mayo in separate bowl. To the mayo add the 1 tsp sugar stir both together really good with fork.

To the mayo and sugar bowl add the whipping cream and begin to stir even more with fork.

To this separate bowl of mayo, sugar and whipping cream add the vinegar and salt.

Add the separate bowl of mayo, sugar, heavy whipping cream, vinegar and salt to all the other ingredients.

Chill and serve, But...

Before serving be sure to say: "this is going to be your favorite"! lol

Once they begin to tell you how great it is; be sure to say thank you and tell them how much everyone loves it every time you make it. (and make sure to leave them wanting more by not making an over abundance of it)

If they begin to ask you for the recipe, let them know they can buy GRANNY NANCY'S RECIPE BOOK. LOL

ENJOY!

A Recipe for help in moving forward

YOU CAN (most of us can) GET AWAY FROM OUR PAST IF WE WANT TO!
CREATE A NEW DAY FOR YOURSELF BY MAKING A CHOICE TO
LEAVE THE PAST IN THE PAST.

Do not, Do not..... LOOK FOR A BETTER YESTERDAY!
IT IS IMPOSSIBLE TO CHANGE YESTERDAY.
TRYING TO CHANGE YESTERDAY IS EQUIVALENT TO
BEATING YOUR HEAD AGAINST A WALL.
YESTERDAY IS HISTORY.
ONCE YOU DECIDE TO LET IT GO
EVERYTHING WILL SEEM BETTER
NOW YOU CAN LIVE FORWARD.

REJOICE!
JOY TO THE WORLD!

TO FINISH THIS SUGGESTION WITH HOPES OF REALLY MAKING
AN IMPACT ON ALL WHO READ MY LIFE OF RECIPES. READ ON
FOR WHAT I HAVE TOLD MY CHILDREN AND GRANDCHILDREN ALL
THEIR LIVES.................

IT IS VERY SIMPLE & VERY HELPFUL....

IN LIFE,
ONLY COUNT THE GOOD
DO NOT COUNT THE BAD

Chicken Rice Salad

(for starters make your Ginger Lemon Dressing first so it can be chilled, see recipe at bottom of page)

3 cups cut up cooked Chicken
2 cups cold cooked Rice
2 cups fresh Pineapple or 1 can (20 ounces) pineapple chunks in juice, drained
¼ cup chopped red Onion
1 medium stalk Celery, chopped (about ½ cup)
1 medium Carrot shredded (about ½ cup)
Lettuce leaves
1 cup Alfalfa Sprouts
2 tablespoons salted Sunflower Seeds (if desired)

Prepare Ginger-Lemon Dressing. (See below)
Mix chicken, rice, pineapple, onion, celery and carrot in a large bowl.
Pour dressing over chicken mixture and toss.

Cover and refrigerate at least 4 hours until chilled.
Serve on Lettuce leaves.
Top with Alfalfa Sprouts.
Sprinkle with Sunflower seeds if (optional)

About 6 servings.

ENJOY!

GINGER LEMON DRESSING

1/3 Cup Olive Oil
3 Tablespoons Lemon Juice
1 Tablespoon Honey
½ Teaspoon ground Ginger
1/8 Teaspoon Garlic or Garlic Powder
4 drops red pepper sauce (optional)

Combine ingredients in a jar with a tight-fitting lid; Shake well. Refrigerate until ready to serve.

ENJOY!

Recipe FOR Health & Leg Cramps

Turmeric! Listen up..........
Yellow Mustard has Turmeric. I say that to say this:
A teaspoon of mustard contains the spice "turmeric" - about a teaspoon of this yellow stuff might help clear out brain cell waste that may play a role in Alzheimer's disease. A little dab also may slash your risk of arthritis and colon cancer, and maybe even help you slim down? Who knows? They are learning more every day.

Oh yeah, Lisa said....My mother in law suggested taking a spoonful or so if you get leg cramps! Crazy, huh? It worked for me! Keep one of those a little packets from the fast food joint by your bed in case you get a cramp in the middle of the night.

Diego Salad

1 large bunch Broccoli (tips only – cut small into individuals)
8 ounces White Mushrooms (sliced)
3 Tomatoes (cut into quarters)
Green OR Red onions chopped (optional)
Black Pepper
Salt

Wash above ingredients, cut up as suggested. Suggestion; if you don't care for raw broccoli you can always put in glass dish with cover and cook for about 2 ½ minutes in microwave. Chill in fridge for about an hour then move forward with recipe.
Rinse mushrooms and dry with paper towels a bit.
Wash Green Onions and chop. (or Red Onions)
Wash and cut tomatoes in chunks that are the same size as the broccoli.
Combine all ingredients together in glass bowl.
Sprinkle with Black pepper and stir together.

Drizzle Dressing over top.

Paul Roger Dressing (for Diego salad)

1/2 cup Mayo
1/2 cup Cocktail sauce –or- chili sauce
1 teaspoon Worcestershire Sauce
1 teaspoon Lemon Juice
1/2 teaspoon Horseradish

Whip with a fork really really good. This is the best dressing you'll ever eat!

ENJOY!

Help Recipe of helpful thoughts for those raising
CHILDREN

- Remember, your children are not your children. They may come through you but not from you. And though they are with you, they don't belong to you. You may give them your love, but not your thoughts, for they have their own thoughts. (check your Bible it will tell you. Our children are a gift from God) GOD ONLY LOANED THEM TO US TO CARE FOR THEM.
-
- Teach your children to tell the truth. Like I have always told my children, tell the truth......God gets the news first. Who do you really think you are fooling when you lie? People? Strangers? They don't even really matter in the end anyway. God has his own agenda for you and like I said he gets the news first. Hellooooooo. (Share this with your children, continuously. All ages, LOL)
-
- About acceptance, I have said to my child; Pass down to your children "acceptance", as it is how you keep the best parts of someone you love alive. Give your child acceptance I gave it to my child. Especially once they are grown, accept them as they are.
-
- You must teach your children to be sensitive about other people's feelings and how what you say or do may impact another person's life. Don't make your children figure this out on their own. (be sure to let them know people remember how someone made them feel)

Dillon Salad
Yields 4 servings

Romaine Lettuce
Light Mozzarella Cheese (shredded)
Avocado
Fresh Blackberries
Fresh Pear cut up
Chives
Tomatoes

Kane Dressing

½ cup Olive Oil
¼ cup Orange Juice
½ Teaspoon Lemon
¼ teaspoon Salt
¼ teaspoon Pepper
½ teaspoon white rice vinegar

ENJOY!

ON LIFE....
Another little recipe......

Why are you waiting for someone else to decide what's going to happen in your life? This can apply to a lot of situations. Just move on, it's better.
Make it happen now!
YOU make it happen.

Granny's Sweet Potato Salad

5 medium Size Sweet Potatoes
½ Cup Dark Raisins
Small Pineapple
1 Sweet Apple
½ teaspoon Cinnamon
½ teaspoon ground Cloves
½ teaspoon nutmeg
1 teaspoon Vanilla
¼ cup Pineapple Juice
1 Lime

Wash Sweet Potatoes – do not peel (unless you want to)
Bake Sweet Potatoes @ 425 for 40 minutes
Check and see if done. (should be somewhat firm – do not over cook) You want to be able to cut in cubes. (now you can peel, it's easier)
Cool off and refrigerate until cold
Cut in cubes
Cut Pineapple in cubes
Cut Apple in little cubes

In little bowl combine all spices together and stir together.

Combine everything and mix together, squeeze lime over all and mix together.

ENJOY!

BIG PHAT Recipe regarding

PAINS FROM YOUR PAST

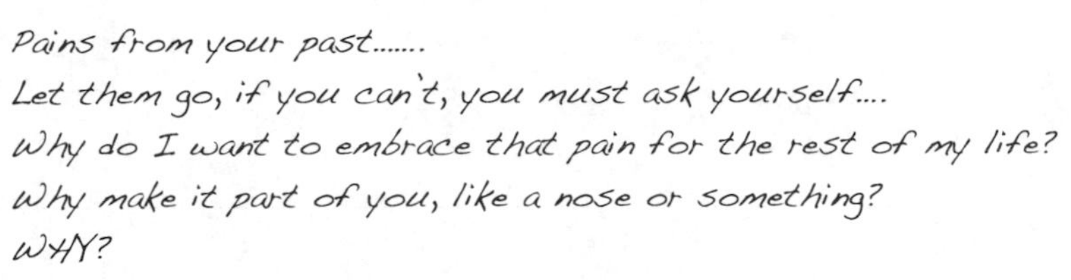

Pains from your past.......
Let them go, if you can't, you must ask yourself....
Why do I want to embrace that pain for the rest of my life?
Why make it part of you, like a nose or something?
WHY?
Is it to make people think; you poor thing, you are suffering? (what good does that do?)
Do you have some odd desire to be a victim?
To get pity?

Is that the reward you give to the people that were there for you? Wow, that's not nice.

You are either going to be bitter or better. You decide. Better is Better!

CELEBRATE THE GOOD (not the bad) Get it?
Let old pains go!
Try it, I promise you will like it Better.

Niko Mandarin Cranberry Salad

2 heads of Romaine lettuce
1 jar of Mandarin Oranges
1 cup dried Cranberries
Handful or so of Lo Mein Noodles
1 cup or so of Pecans (first put in bowl, drizzle olive oil, sprinkle sugar, stir and put in oven for 10 minutes or so @ 350 degrees)

Dressing

1 cup Olive Oil
Juice from a ½ of a Lemon
½ cup Orange Juice
¼ teaspoon Pepper
¼ teaspoon Salt
Garlic (cut big pieces and soak in Dressing then remove)

Recipe from old friend

ENJOY!

JUST A THOUGHT.................

I just read an article that was so nutty it was comical.

It said:
Researchers discovered lack of exercise, constant snacking, over eating, eating fried foods and foods with sugar = WEIGHT GAIN. Which in turn equals obesity? Wow! I wonder how much tax money was spent researching these stark discoveries?
Hmmmmm..........what do you think? LOL Just something to think about.

I mean, didn't we all already know that? LOL

Shrimp Pasta Salad

This salad is served best when cold.

2 pounds Cooked Shrimp
1 ½ cup Zucchini, very thinly sliced
1 ½ cup fresh white Mushrooms, sliced
1 medium Red Onion, thinly sliced
½ cup fresh Parmesan Cheese
1 bag Rotini Pasta
1 Lemon
1 tablespoon Olive oil
Garlic Powder
Salt
Pepper

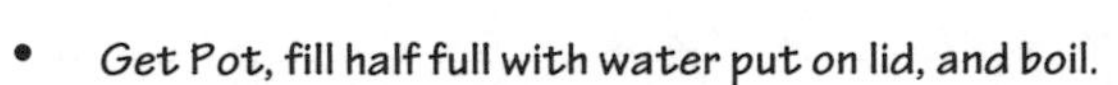

- Get Pot, fill half full with water put on lid, and boil.
- Once boiling, add Rotini Pasta and cook as instructed on package. (DO NOT OVERCOOK PASTA)
- Once cooked, drain and set aside to cool off.
- Rinse Shrimp, set aside in colander to drain.
- Squeeze Lemon over Shrimp and set aside again.
- Wash all vegetables
- Slice up vegetables as suggested above.
- Combine all together and toss.
- Add Olive Oil
- Season with a little Garlic Powder, Salt, and Pepper TOSS and...............

ENJOY!

CHILDREN AND PARENTING
Recipes on life...

Here's a lot of info from Life experience........
....

Proper motherhood has great rewards – but don't expect it as nothing is guaranteed except Gods love.

You cannot protect your child from mean people. What you can do is: You CAN demonstrate to them how to handle different situations.

Children; Their failure is your failure (sometimes) So put the effort in.

Please remember; when our children are young we must give them rules to live by and we must be very strong and consistent about enforcing those rules. There is no turning back the hands of time. Period. You don't get to start all over.

When punishing your children, give penalty's and maybe take away privileges. You want your children to have fear of your power not your strength. CAPSIYHE?

A lot of people only make time for what is important to themselves, this is called "self serving" behavior. Are you making time for the things that are important to your kids? Ask them to tell you what they want to do with 30 minutes of your time. Make them happy and give them memories. Remember , we don't know if we have tomorrow.........?

Don't expect anything out of your kids that you don't expect out of yourself!

You cannot beat your child into being a better version of their-self! Helloooooo! Just sayin!

Mikhail Spinach Salad

Amounts will be based on number of people……so go for it!

Ingredients for Salad and Dressing:
Fresh Baby Spinach
Romaine Lettuce
Avocado – sliced
Red Onions – sliced
Blue Berries
Raisins
Olive Oil
1 Lemon
Salt
Pepper
Paprika
Garlic Powder

Rinse your spinach and romaine lettuce and lay in colander to drain. You can pat dry with paper towels if you like.
Cut avocado in half and slice.
Peel red onion and slice.
Rinse blueberries and let drain in colander.

Cut spinach and romaine lettuce into bite size pieces and put in large salad bowl along with avocado, red onion, blueberries and raisins and toss around.

Special Dressing

(You'll need an old jar or a container with a secure lid so you can shake real well)

Mix the following ingredients:

½ cup Olive Oil
1 teaspoon Lemon
1 teaspoon Rice Vinegar
¼ teaspoon Salt
¼ teaspoon Pepper
¼ teaspoon Garlic Powder
¼ teaspoon Paprika
*Optional – 1 tablespoon Heated Bacon drippings YUM!
If you want a little extra spicy kick – Add 1/8 teaspoon red pepper

-Or-

Sprinkle some Red Pepper Flakes in the Salad (OPTIONAL)

ENJOY!

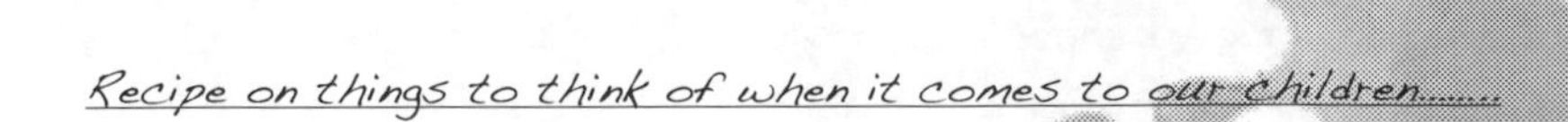

Recipe on things to think of when it comes to our children.......

We must remember there are things in life that adults have a difficult time dealing with such as; divorce, relocation, finances, death, relationship issues etc. etc. If these things are difficult for us as adults can you just imagine how a child or even a young person must be feeling when they have to deal with things that they don't understand yet? They don't have life experience! Please remember that. So when you move and change their schools & friends and everything they are familiar with, remember to ask them how they're doing. They don't even know that certain feelings are only temporary. So don't be frustrated when a child's behavior changes because so many things are happening. Be understanding. Pay attention, please. Make it a point to not let your children know your adult problems. Trust me, they do hear you talking on the phone, you think they are not paying attention yet trust me, when you think they are watching TV, playing Video games, doing their iPod, Seriously? They are always always listening even when you don't think so. They are very clever at not making eye contact-but storing information. (CHILDREN are the #1 multi taskers these days)

Also, listen up.....................for those of you having behavior problems from your child/children ....

You wonder why your children misbehave? Well, you allowed them to make their own decisions because it was easier to be flexible and give them their way at the time, than sticking to your guns. (you may be on the phone a lot or pre-occupied or you simply don't make time for them) So they just make their own decisions, then you wonder why they are not the same decisions "you" might have made). Really? They are young. You basically let them make their own rules. Seriously??? Hellooooo.

Have a family meeting and write down what is going to change from this day forward. You will be surprised how children appreciate a family meeting and see it as official and may possibly be more inclined to follow structure. (they love structure and consistency, they just don't know how to say it)
BTW..."Family" sometimes is only 2 of you, so you can still have a family meeting, Capishe?

Dominique Salad

Ingredients:

Amounts will be your choice…..and be sure to wash the fruits & Veggies, ok?

Romaine Lettuce
fresh Baby Spinach
Crabmeat (you can use canned crab or imitation crab,)
Green Onions
Fresh Blueberries
Cherry Tomatoes
Cucumbers

Niko Dressing

¾ cup of Salad Oil (aka vegetable oil -or- olive oil is good too)
¼ cup Rice Vinegar (or wine vinegar)
A pinch of Salt
A pinch of Pepper
¼ Orange Juice
MIX ALL TOGETHER IN A GLASS JAR OR ANYTHING WITH A LID BECAUSE YOU WILL NEED TO "shake" "shake" "shake" !!!!

ENJOY!

Salad – That's not so Lettucy
This is called "Shay" salad. (*_*)

Ingredients:

4 boneless Chicken Breast (cut off all fat)
1 Romaine lettuce head (must be romaine)
¼ cup red Onion (diced)
1 Avocado
5 Roma Tomatoes
1 can Green Peas
¾ cup Blueberries
3 Carrots (shredded)

Preheat oven to 450
Rinse chicken breast
Pat chicken breast dry with paper towel
Sprinkle with salt and pepper (very very lightly)
Arrange chicken in large baking dish 1 inch apart
Bake for 25 minutes
Check for doneness by cutting through thickest part of chicken and confirm there is no pink juices.
If so.....bake for another 4 minutes. Check again, but do not leave chicken unattended at this point as even 1 minute could cause it to be overdone. Ok?
Once chicken is done, set aside to cool off.
After cooled off, cut in 1 inch squares.

While chicken is cooking:
Rinse lettuce and layout on paper towels to dry, don't use the whole head.
Once lettuce is dry................
Cross cut (you know like a criss cross paper shredder would – cut really small)
Peel red onion and dice (this means little squares, lol)
Avocado – wash and slice down the center, remove seed. (be careful removing seed) cut in big chunks.
Wash tomatoes and cut in medium chunks
Open green pea's and drain all juice.
Rinse blueberries lightly and let drain.
Shred carrots with cheese grater.

Ok........combine all ingredients in large bowl.
(add peas and avocado's last because you don't want them to get mashed too much as you toss the salad)

Continued on next page......................................

DRESSING FOR NOT SO LETTUCY SALAD
("Shay" Dressing)

Of course you can use any dressing of your choice, but the following is a favorite.

¾ cup Olive oil
¼ cup Flavored Vinegar
½ teaspoon Salt
½ teaspoon Pepper
1Teaspoon Sugar

Combine olive oil and vinegar together first in a jar and shake really really good. Then add the remaining ingredients and continue to shake really good before pouring.

SHAKE! SHAKE! AND SHAKE! THIS SALAD DRESSING TAKES A LOT OF SHAKING.

ENJOY!

Recipe on People in your Life

The people that you want in your life will show you that they want you in their life too. If they don't initiate calls and make contact like you do, think about that? It's called reciprocation. Sometimes you love people and nothing comes back? For what? If you have to beg, Forget about it! (in other words, don't keep hurting your own feelings)

Jevon Salad

My recipe makes a big bowl.

Mix all the ingredients below together in a bowl.

Add more, Add less- your preference.

One head of romaine lettuce, diced.

2 cups of grape tomatoes, halved.

One cucumber, sliced thinly.

One Yellow and one red bell pepper, sliced, not diced.

Half an onion, sliced.

Half a cup of kalamata olives.

Crumbled Feta cheese.

Oregano, salt and pepper to season.

LEMON AND OIL DRESSING
(this is a very small amount, like for 1 salad)

Ingredients:

½ small garlic clove, finely mined
1 teaspoon sea salt
3 tablespoons extra-virgin olive oil
1 Tablespoon freshly squeezed lemon juice

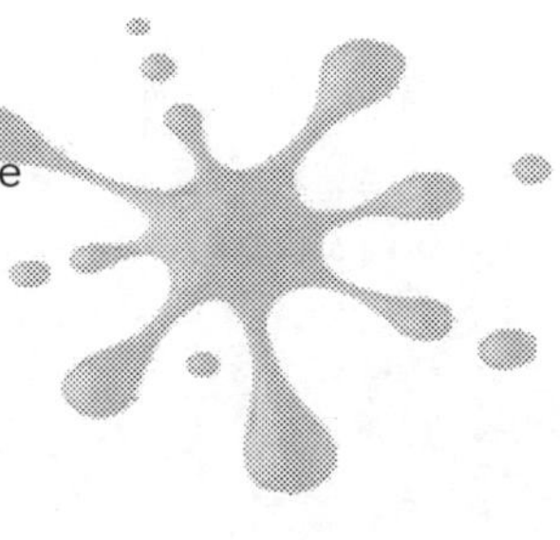

ENJOY!

123 CAESAR SALAD

1 package Romaine Lettuce (wash and drain in colander while shredding chicken)

1 Rotisserie Chicken, Shredded (just pick up an already cooked one at the store)

Caesar Dressing (get pre made at store – get the one in the refrigerated section)

Parmesan Croutons

1 Package Shredded Parmesan Cheese (from refrigerated shredded cheese section in the store)

Toss all the above ingredients together in large bowl and serve.

ENJOY!

Warm Spinach Salad

Ingredients:

Fresh Baby Spinach (have a large amount as spinach cooks down to a very little amount)
Red Onion
Roma Tomatoes (or what ever kind you like)
Avocados
Black Berries
Lemon
Olive Oil (light extra virgin)
Salt
Pepper
Garlic Powder

Cut Red Onion however you like and set aside.
Cut Lemon and set aside.

Cut Avocado and salt and pepper it and sprinkle with lemon and set aside. CONTINUED NEXT PAGE.....
Cut Tomatoes in medium bite size pieces, sprinkle with salt and pepper and drizzle with a bit of olive oil and garlic powder and toss. (very light on the garlic powder)

Now.......Get a large pot and have the lid nearby. Also have a large cooking spoon nearby,

Pour in some Olive Oil. No need to cover the entire bottom of the pan.
Turn your burner on low and immediately add the Spinach. DO NOT LEAVE UNATTENDED as you will be cooking it for less than 4 minutes.

As the Spinach cooks down, add more spinach as now you will have more room in your pan. Add Pepper and if needed another dash of Olive Oil and continuously keep mixing together. Do not overcook. Once it is SLIGHTLY cooked, turn off burner and place lid on the pan.

Now get your individual salad bowls and spoon Spinach into the bowl then begin to layer all the rest of the ingredients in the order you like.

This is healthy and Tasty!

ENJOY!

RECIPE TO BE GRATEFUL

Acknowledge that you have everything by recognizing all those that have so little.
Be Grateful

HONEY DIJON SALAD AND DRESSING

Ingredients:

Baby Spinach
Sliced Mushrooms
Red Onions – diced
Blackberries
Blueberries
Tomatoes
Avocado

Wash and slice all the above ingredients, set aside and make the dressing below:

Honey Dijon Dressing

1 cup of nonfat plain yogurt
1 ½ Tbsp Dijon mustard
2 Tbsp honey

FLAXSEED OIL DRESSING

¾ cup Flaxseed Oil
¼ Cup Red Wine Vinegar
½ Tsp Dijon mustard
½ tsp maple syrup
½ tsp crushed garlic
½ tsp oregano

Combine all ingredients together and shake really good.

ENJOY!

ORANGE POPPY SEED DRESSING

Ingredients:

½ cup nonfat plain yogurt
¼ cup Orange Juice concentrate, thawed
2 tbsp Poppy Seeds
1 Tablespoon Honey

Combine all ingredients together and shake really good.

ENJOY!

SOY GINGER SESAME DRESSING

Ingredients:

½ cup nonfat Sour Cream
1 ½ tbsp light Soy Sauce
3 Tbsp Rice Wine Vinegar
2 Tsp minced Garlic
1 Tbsp Stevia
1 Tbsp Sesame Seeds

Combine all ingredients together and shake really good.

ENJOY!

AVOCADO OIL & VINEGAR DRESSING

Ingredients:

¼ cup Avocado Oil
1 Tbsp Rice Vinegar
1 Tbsp Honey
Juice of 1 Lemon
¼ Tsp Sea Salt

Combine all ingredients together and shake really good.

ENJOY!

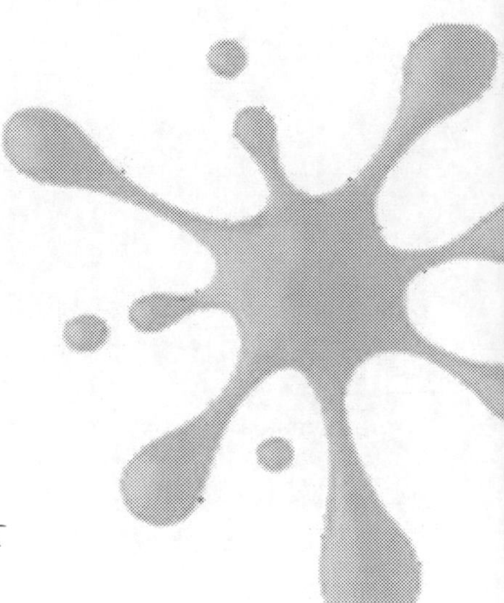

Recipe on carrying EMOTIONAL BAGGAGE

Don't carry your emotional baggage in a Big Giant Green Trash bag weighing down your precious shoulders! Tuck your emotional baggage into a Tiny little zip lock bag and be done with it.

Move on, it's better. Another situation where it is your choice to let go. Nobody likes trash, it serves no purpose. Don't bring it into potential relationships. Don't drag all that baggage through life. (remember, don't look for a better ending for yesterday)

Just sayin...........

Recipe for Single Women who Date

I am going to be blunt.

Do not let him try you out! (you know what I mean)

Recipe for a Lasting, Loving, Happy Marriage

Ask yourself everyday; What can I do for my spouse?

Make it a GOAL to do more for your spouse than your spouse does for you,

Eventually it will become a game, because each will want to be the winner at doing the most for the other. Winning feels good! Having a Happy Spouse feels even better!

Remember that if you don't have a PLAN, it is merely a WISH..............

Plain old "wishful thinking" doesn't usually come to fruition.

Make your spouse NUMBER ONE, Just as you promised God in your vows.

Just sayin..

Various Breakfasts and Breads

EGGS
BREADS
BISCUITS
PANCAKES
APPLE FLAP JACKS
BREAKFAST BREAD
FRUIT DISH
MAKE IT YOURSELF PANCAKE SYRUP

BREADS

These are quick breads to make.

TWO Big TIPS to make Bread successfully are:

***Be accurate with the measurements!!!!!
***Don't mix the batter too much. (or your bread is going to be tough! just sayin.)
When adding the liquid, stir until the dry ingredients are just moistened; "yes", the batter will be lumpy, Capishe?

MICRO WAVE BRAN MUFFIN

This makes 1 muffin in 50 seconds.
BELLY FAT CURE
From Dr. Oz Show

1 Coffee Cup
¼ Cup Ground Flax
1 TSP Baking Powder
2 TSP Cinnamon
2 Packets Stevia
1 TSP Coconut Oil
1 Egg
1 Tablespoon overflowing with Applesauce (optional)

Mix all Dry ingredients together in a Big Coffee Cup
Microwave on High for 50 seconds

Once microwave is complete, let sit in there for about a minute and then take out and dump onto plate and cut into a couple of slices. YUM! It should come out very easily and it will look like a Biscuit.

Enjoy!

Scrambled Eggs
Secret tips

Ok, so nobody likes spongy, browned, overcooked eggs, right? So follow my little suggestions and it will be a no brainer.

Ingredients:

Eggs
Butter

Things you will need:
A nonstick skillet or a cast-iron pan.
A heat-proof spatula or a flat topped wooden spoon or last but not least chopsticks. (just not a fork!)
Capishe?

Crack your eggs into a clear glass bowl of some sort, so you can see clearly that a piece of shell didn't get in there accidentally. If so, scoop it out with a piece of the bigger shell. (the little piece of shell is too hard to get out with your fingers -it will run from your fingers.......but it will be attracted to go back into its original shell, get a piece of the empty shell and scoop it out -try it and you will see. A lot of people don't know this but Granny Nancy does) smile
Put your butter in your pan and let it begin to melt on a lower medium setting. (we don't' want burnt butter flavor, capishe?)

Now, whisk them really vigorously – you want to add air and volume for really fluffy eggs. Whisk the eggs right before adding them to the pan; don't whisk and let the mixture sit (it deflates).

Do NOT add milk, cream or water to the eggs. This will cause problems and you will not have fluffy eggs. Got it?

Do NOT use high heat. It is all about patience if you want wonderful fluffy eggs. If you want large fluff – stir but stir less, You need to scramble eggs over medium-low heat, pull the pan off the heat if it gets too hot, until they set to desired thickness. So basically, remove the pan from the heat before you think they are done as the pan will carry over heat and they will keep cooking for a minute or so anyway.

You now have Wonderful Fluffy Scrambled Eggs to **ENJOY!**

1-2-3 Banana Bread

Preheat Oven to 350

Ingredients:

½ cup unsalted Butter
¾ cup granulated Sugar
1 Egg
2 cups all-purpose Flour
2 teaspoons Baking Powder
¾ cup whole Milk
1 large Banana, mashed
1/3 cup unsalted Butter, melted
½ cup light Brown Sugar
1 cup canned crushed Pineapple, drained
Whipped cream, to serve

Preheat the oven to 350. Grease six small glass dishes of some sort OR 6 small springform cake pans OR an 8 – inch springform cake pan.

Beat the butter, sugar, and egg until smooth. Sift in the flour and baking powder. Mix well, then add the milk and mashed banana.

Spread the melted butter in the base of each tin, then sprinkle evenly with the brown sugar.

Spread the crushed pineapple over the sugar. Pour the batter evenly over the top. Bake for 40 minutes.

After cooling off for 10 minutes, unmold onto plate. (do not let it stay in pan too long or it will stick to pan)

Serve with Whipped Cream.

ENJOY!

PUMPKIN BREAD

Pre heat oven to 350

3 cups Sugar
1 cup cooking Oil
4 Eggs
3 1/3 cups all-purpose Flour
2 teaspoons baking soda
1 ½ teaspoons Salt
1 teaspoon ground Cinnamon
1 teaspoon ground Nutmeg
2/3 cup Water
1 15-ounce can pumpkin

Grease the bottom and ½ inch up the sides of three 8 x 4 x 2-inch or
Four 7 ½ x 3 ½ x 2 inch loaf pans and then set aside.
In a large mixing bowl beat Sugar and Oil with an electric mixer on medium speed.

Add eggs and beat well; set aside.

In a large mixing bowl combine flour, soda, salt, cinnamon and nutmeg.

Add dry mixture and water alternately to sugar mixture, beating on low speed after each addition just until combined. Beat in pumpkin.

Spoon batter into prepared pans. Bake in a 350 oven 55 to 60 minutes or until wooden toothpick inserted in centers comes out clean.

Cool completely on wire racks. Wrap and store overnight before slicing.

ENJOY!

RECIPE TO MOVE ON TO ANOTHER STEP IN YOUR LIFE

I always say there are certain steps we all need to complete in life and if we don't complete each one successfully then we cannot move on to the next step. Hence......the reason why some people never move on. (Keep this thought in mind to help encourage yourself or someone else to complete things). Be it relationships, projects etc etc. If you deem it complete then even that is enough if you gave it everything you got. Capishe?

Angel Biscuits

This recipe will make about 1 dozen.

(This dough can be kept for up to three days in a covered bowl in the fridge)

2 ½ cups Flour
2 Tablespoons White Sugar
½ Teaspoon Salt
½ Teaspoon Baking Powder
¾ cup Warm buttermilk
½ Cup Shortening
¼ cup warm Water
1 - .25 package active dry yeast

Dissolve the yeast in the warm water; set aside.
Mix the dry ingredients in the order given, cutting in the shortening as you normally do for biscuits or pie dough.
Stir the buttermilk into the yeast and water mixture and mix thoroughly. The dough is ready to refrigerate.

When it is time to make them:

Remove dough, put on floured surface. Knead dough about 15 times and form it into a ball.

Turn the dough out on a floured board and knead lightly. Roll out to about a ¾ thickness and cut with a biscuit cutter into about 2 -1/2 inches, placing them in a greased pan. Cover the dough and let it rise until it pretty much doubles for about 40 minutes or so.

After letting dough rise before baking, bake at 400 F oven for about 12-14 minutes.

ENJOY!

Recipe to understand Circumstances in your Life

God engineers all circumstances - not man.
It is the loyal soul that knows this.
My loyalty is to our Lord.
You decide where your loyalty is.

Nancy's Instant Bread Muffin
My husband calls it:
"Nancy Cutie Pie Bread)

Makes 1 Muffin. (~_~)

You will need:

A microwave
1 really large coffee cup
¼ cup regular flour
1 Teaspoon Baking Powder
2 Packets of Stevia
1 Teaspoon Coconut Oil
1 overflowing Tablespoon Apple Sauce
1 Egg

In your coffee cup stir 1 egg really good.
To the egg, add 1 Teaspoon Coconut Oil.
To the egg and the Coconut Oil, Add 1 huge tablespoon of Applesauce and 2 packets of Stevia.

Now, you will add the Baking powder. With your fork whip it all really good and then add the flour and continue to stir up really good.

Leave it all in the coffee cup and pop the coffee cup in microwave for 65 seconds,
After 65 seconds, take it out and immediately dump out of coffee cup onto little plate and "Abra Kadabra" POOF ! You have a cute Bread Biscuit, cut it in half, butter it up and it will melt in your mouth!

ENJOY!

A tip to remember........

When you find yourself telling the same sad story about you or your life over and over, then let it go as there is no benefit in it. Remember, everybody has a story so let it go. Don't dwell on it. Stop reliving it. It is better for you to let it go so you can be happy. Remember this: "Trying to change the past would be like trying to eat applesauce with chopsticks"? What kind of sense would that make? Helloooooooooo

Zucchini Bread
Pre heat oven to 350 degrees
I have had this recipe for a long time.

Ingredients:

3 ¼ cups all-purpose flour
1 ½ Teaspoons Salt
1 Teaspoon Nutmeg
2 Teaspoons Baking Soda
1 Teaspoon Cinnamon
3 cups Sugar
1 cup Vegetable Oil
4 Eggs, beaten
1/3 cups water
2 cups grated Zucchini
1 Teaspoon Lemon Juice
1 cup chopped walnuts or pecans (optional)

In a large bowl combine flour, salt, nutmeg, baking soda, cinnamon and sugar.
In another bowl combine the oil, eggs, water, zucchini and lemon juice.
Mix wet ingredients into dry ingredients.

Bake in loaf pans (probably 2 loaf pans will work) BAKE FOR 1 HOUR.
OR
Bake in about 5 or 6 mini loaf pans. BAKE FOR ABOUT 45 MINUTES.

EITHER WAY, TEST WITH A FORK IN CENTER AND IF THE FORK COMES OUT CLEAN IT IS DONE!

ENJOY!

APPLE FLAPJACKS

Ingredients you will need:

- 1 tablespoon Shortening
- 1 tablespoon Sugar
- 2 Eggs
- 1 ½ cups sifted Flour
- 1 teaspoon Baking Powder
- ½ teaspoon Cinnamon
- 1 cup Apples, chopped fine
- 1 cup Milk

Cream shortening and sugar.
Add beaten eggs, sifted flour, with baking powder.
Add cinnamon & chopped apples.
Then add milk gradually to make a medium batter.
Bake on griddle as you would for ordinary pancakes and serve in an overlapping row around a platter of pork chops or serve separately with roast pork.

Makes 16.

ENJOY!

HOMEMADE PANCAKE SYRUP

¾ cup Brown Sugar
¼ cup Sugar
¾ cup Water
½ cup Honey
½ Teaspoon Vanilla

Combine, heat a bit and **ENJOY!**

Lionel's PANCAKES FROM SCRATCH

Ingredients you will need:

- 2 cups Flour
- 1 ¾ cups Milk
- 2 tablespoons Baking Powder
- 2 Eggs, beat them separately before adding to mixture
- ¼ cup Butter, melted (1/8 of a pound)
- 3 tablespoons Sugar
- 1 teaspoon Salt

Mix dry items first
Combine the eggs and melted butter to the milk and slowly stir in the flour.
Let sit at least 10 minutes while heating the pan.
These will be high, but light and fluffy..........

This recipe makes "9" 6 inch pancakes **ENJOY!**

By Brother William

Good Recipe to Change yourself....
Well, good motivation at the least....
Listen up.....

Who we are today is not necessarily who we are going to be tomorrow. SO IT'S ALL GOOD. There is always hope.

BIG PHAT TIP

Remember this.........
Physical training is of value.........BUT
Godliness training is soooo much more valuable for your present life and the life to come.

Big Fat Baked Pancake
(2 to 4 Servings)

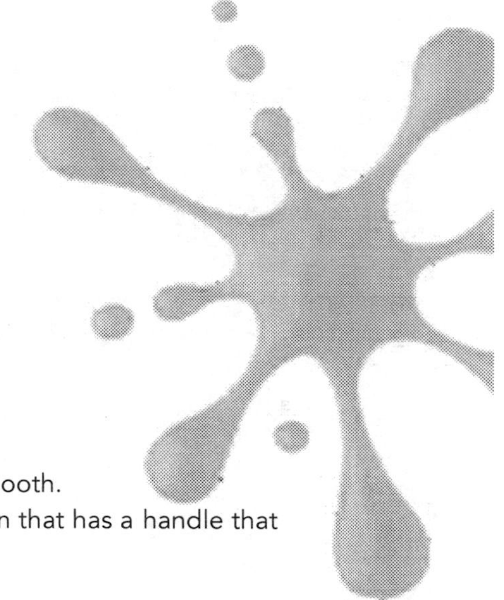

Ingredients you will need:

- 2 Large Eggs, beaten slightly
- Pinch of Salt
- ½ cup of Milk
- ½ cup All-purpose Flour, sifted
- Pinch Of ground Nutmeg
- 1 tablespoon unsalted Butter
- Powdered Sugar

Preheat oven to 425 degrees.
In a medium bowl, whisk together eggs, salt milk, flour and nutmeg until smooth.
Melt butter in a 10 inch cast iron skillet over medium heat. (or any frying pan that has a handle that won't melt in the oven)
Pour batter into pan.
Place in oven and bake uncovered for 10 to 12 minutes until pancake is puffed and edges are brown.
Serve immediately with powdered sugar or what ever else you like!

I usually cut it into pieces with a pizza cutter.

ENJOY!

Change yourself Recipe....

REMEMBER THIS ALWAYS.........

When you change the way you look at things....................
The things you look at change......

Just sayin................

Blueberry Breakfast Bread

Yields 16 (makes 2 loaves)

Ingredients:

1 cup (2 sticks) Butter, melted, plus additional butter for greasing two loaf pans.
1 ½ cup Blueberries
3 /1/2 cups Flour, divided
4 teaspoons Baking Powder
½ teaspoon Salt
½ teaspoon Baking Soda
2 cups Sugar
4 large Eggs
1 cup Milk
2 teaspoons Vanilla

Heat the oven to 375 degrees and grease two 8 inch loaf pans with butter. Line the bottom of each pan with parchment paper, and grease the top of the parchment paper with butter.

Wash the blueberries and drain. Lightly dry with a paper towel and place in a small bowl. Toss the berries with 2 tablespoons of the flour to coat. Set aside.

Place the remaining flour into a large mixing bowl and whisk in the baking powder, salt, baking soda and sugar. Set aside.

In a medium bowl, whisk the eggs, then whisk in the milk and vanilla. Finally, whisk in the 1 cup of melted butter.

Make a well in the center of the dry ingredients, and pour in the liquid ingredients. Stir the ingredients together lightly just to combine; do not over mix the batter. Lastly, gently fold in the berries.

Fill the loaf pan evenly; they should be just over half full.

Place the pans in the oven and bake until done, about 50 minutes.

Check the bread every 10 minutes after 30 minutes; if it begins to color too quickly, tent it lightly with aluminum foil.

Once done, cool and serve.

ENJOY!

Whipped BlueBerry Beauty Breakfast Snack

Freeze Fresh Blueberries
After Frozen – rinse off and drain in colander
Put a cereal bowl size amount of Blueberries in cereal bowl (or bowl of your choice of course)

Now...........

Top with Whipped Cream!

ENJOY!

Recipe to have compassion for
those that suffer from
Depression:

KNOW AND UNDERSTAND THIS AS IT IS NOT AS SIMPLE AS YOU THINK.....
Sadness is an emotion, OK?
ON THE OTHER HAND.......
Depression is an chemistry thing, people can't help that.
(People need to know this to have compassion for those with depression)
REACH OUT AND UNDERSTAND

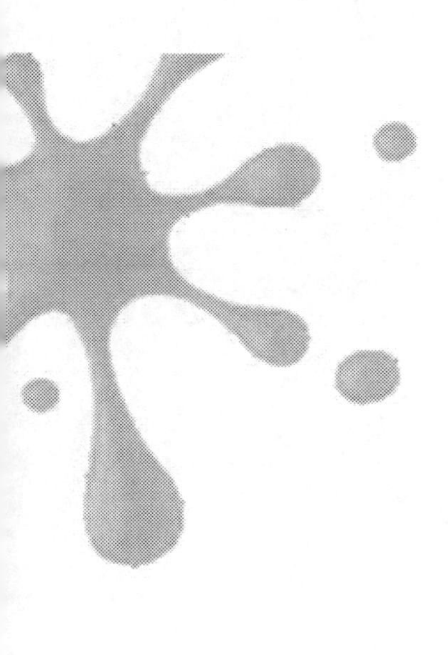

Recipe to not buy into feeling bad for the person that is basically mistreating you.
Verbal abuse applies.....

Here is something to think about..................

Those of you that get emotionally abused by husbands, wives, friends, relatives, co-workers, bosses etc. Think about this:

After being beat up physically, emotionally, verbally or otherwise.
Why do you feel bad for the person who is trying to make you feel bad?? STOP THAT!!!!!
Think about that! Stop it, don't let yourself play into that! Emotional abuse means that.... that person possibly doesn't care about you. Avoid them as much as possible. Most of all.....do not feel sorry for them. Don't let them flip the script on you either. Watch these types of people carefully. You hear all your life about people that are 2 faced. Well, these type of people I'm talking about have many sides to their face not just two.
Be careful, when there are more than 2 sides to someone's face then you must be very careful. Limit your time around these types of people. Protect yourself, you are responsible for your feelings. You must care for yourself. Capishe?

More valuable info on dating......................especially 1st dates.

Here is how to operate in those situations......

Remember at all times when you meet someone new - you are in unchartered waters. That being said, in the beginning when you are on dates, these dates should be in public. Also, it is much better to have "safety dates". Safety dates are lunchtime dates which obviously are during the day. The "safety date" is a great thing because 1 hour is enough time to determine if there is an attraction or not and then you can get a little interview in and decide if you even want to go on a 2nd date. The good thing is, you can escape if you want to because you can tell the person you have to get back to work. Right? Capishe! (Plus you can meet at a restaurant and then bounce) Oh and go dutch because it is fair and it eliminates any feelings of obligation.

Daytime dates have a whole different ambiance - you will not end the date with a false sense of someone because most likely there won't be a fantasy atmosphere. (Liquor can create that and consequently often we look at others differently when a "mood adjuster" is part of the equation). Ultimately it causes people to look at that person another way. Someone we may not usually choose all of a sudden becomes an option because your standards change when you have a bit of liquor. This is not good. Hence, another reason for safety date.

There you have it! This really simplifies things in the crazy world of dating. Of course this is if you are dating with the intent of looking for someone as a potential mate. If so....that is what dating is for - to get to know someone and to see if there is chemistry of any kind and/or potential - and then again, you know if a second date is in order. Right? Also remember, don't play with people's feelings. Now of course, if you are dating for a sport or a hobby then I don't know what to tell you.

Crockpot Oatmeal Recipe

- 2 cups Steel cut Oats (not instant)
- 4 cups Water
- 1 tsp. Cinnamon
- 1/2 cup Brown Sugar
- 1 tsp. Vanilla
- 2 cups chopped Red Apples, peeled and diced
- 1 cup Raisins
- Pinch of Salt
  - Place all ingredients in Crock Pot.
  - Set on Low temperature setting.
  - Cook 8 to 9 hours.
  - Stir before serving.

If you want to simplify, just include Oats, Water, Salt and Apples. (or just raisins and no Apples)

ENJOY!

MORE ON DATING

Be honest with your dates. - People cannot make good decisions if they don't have the facts to work with. We can all make better decisions when we have the facts. So don't have expectations from the person you have lied to. It's that simple. Write that down too.

Nancy's Good Manner Recipe

Good manners are basically based on kindness, so there you have it. There would be no reason you could say you didn't know any better.
Just Be Kind.

Health Recipe
WARNING

A dirty house is hazardous to the health of your kids!
(and everyone else for that matter)
Germs! Germs! Germs!

FRENCH OR JELLY PANCAKES

Ingredients you will need:

3 Eggs, separated
1 teaspoon Sugar
½ teaspoon Salt
1 cup Milk
2 teaspoons Baking Powder
1 Egg
1 tablespoon melted Shortening

Beat egg yolks.

Add sugar, salt and ½ cup of milk.
Add flour and shortening and mix until smooth.
Add remaining milk.
Fold in stiffly beaten egg whites.
Bake on hot griddle, making cakes larger than usual and very thin.
Spread with jelly and roll up while hot.
Serve with overlapping edges of cakes on bottom to keep them from unrolling.
Sprinkle with confectioner's sugar if desired.
Makes 12

Passed down from relative..........

ENJOY!

Blueberries and Watermelons with Pear Sauce

If you like, you can use ripe peaches, or whatever fruit you might choose and use the nectar from it.

Pear Sauce:

2 ripe Pears
¼ cup Pear Nectar CONTINUED NEXT PAGE...

Ingredients:

4 Watermelon Wedges, each 2 to 3 inches wide
1 cup Blueberries

Here's what you do..................

To make the sauce, peel the pears and cut in half and remove core. Put in Blender or and add some pear nectar, mix until smooth – around 1 minute.

Put a watermelon wedge on each plate. Put about a ¼ cup of the Blueberries over each wedge. Drizzle Pear sauce over the top

ENJOY!

Miss Sweets Christmas Morning Treat
from Aunt Carol
Heat oven to 350

1 grand can of Pillsbury Crescent dinner rolls
2 8 oz. packages of Cream Cheese
1 ½ cups Sugar
1 teaspoon Cinnamon
1 stick of Butter

Soften cream cheese @ room temperature.
Melt butter.
Mix cinnamon with sugar (mix well).
Roll out two of the rolls, place in glass oblong oven baking dish.
Spread cream cheese over those two rolls with rubber spatula.
Sprinkle sugar cinnamon mix over those two rolls.
Place 2 more rolls on top of the above.
Sprinkle sugar cinnamon mix over top two rolls.
Drizzle melted butter over top.

Bake for 30 minutes and **ENJOY!**

RECIPE TO RECOGNIZE WRONG LOVE
(UGLY LOVE)

Ugly love, you know what it is... stay away from it! UGLY LOVE HURTS.
A lot of time it is disguised as real love......if you have to question it - it is ugly. Trust me.
DON'T PUT YOURSELF THROUGH IT.
PEOPLE THAT GIVE UGLY LOVE ARE ONLY GOING TO HURT YOU. (They are usually A self serving type of person = they only think of themselves)

The Paradoxical Commandments
Everyone should read this "often"

For more than thirty years, the Paradoxical Commandments have circled the globe. They have been put on walls and refrigerator doors, featured in speeches and articles, preached from pulpits, and shared extensively on the web. They have been used by business leaders, military commanders, government officials, religious leaders, university presidents, social workers, teachers, rock stars, parents, coaches, and students. Mother Teresa thought the Paradoxical Commandments were important enough to put up on the wall of her children's home in Calcutta.

The Paradoxical Commandments have touched the hearts of millions of people all over the world.

People are illogical, unreasonable, and self-centered.
Love them anyway.

If you do good, people will accuse you of selfish ulterior motives. "Do good anyway."
If you are successful, you will win false friends and true enemies.

Succeed anyway.

The good you do today will be forgotten tomorrow.
Do good anyway.

Honesty and frankness make you vulnerable.
Be honest and frank anyway.

The biggest men and women with the biggest ideas can be shot down by the smallest men and women with the smallest minds.
Think big anyway.

People favor underdogs but follow only top dogs.

Fight for a few underdogs anyway.

What you spend years building may be destroyed overnight.
Build anyway.

People really need help but may attack you if you do help them.
Help people anyway.

Give the world the best you have and you'll get kicked in the teeth.
Give the world the best you have anyway.

By: Kent M. Keith

VEGETABLE & POTATO DISHES

MASHED CARROTS

YES! YOU READ THAT RIGHT!
WHY DOESN'T EVERYBODY KNOW ABOUT THIS? LOL

This is a great recipe to have something different.
Everybody will love it, trust me.

Ingredients:

3 pounds carrots, peeled and cut into chunks
4 Tablespoons (1/2 stick) Butter
½ cup Milk
1 Teaspoon ground Cumin
Salt and ground Black Pepper

In a medium saucepan over high heat, bring 1 inch of water to a boil. Add the carrots, then cover the pot, reduce heat.
Use a slotted spoon to transfer the carrots to a food processor.

Add the butter, milk and cumin, then process until very smooth, about 2 to 3 minutes. You will need to stop the processor and scrape down the sides of the bowl two or three times during processing. When the Carrots resemble mashed potatoes, season with salt and pepper.

If you prefer a smoother or looser consistency, more milk can be added during processing.

(this will make 6 servings)

ENJOY!

MY OPINION

My opinion IS.........

The virtues of family bonds include, Depth, Continuity, and Passionate Loyalty.

A SWEEEEET WAY TO DO SWEET POTATOES

These sweeeeet potatoes are great for us because we don't add all that junk to them that we usually do. Check it out!

Set oven to 450 degrees

4 Large Sweet Potatoes
3 Fresh Limes
5 Tablespoons Light Olive Oil

Wash Sweet Potatoes really good, remove anything from outer skin that looks like something you don't want to eat. But pretty much leave the skin on. (It taste good and it's good for you)

Ok.........now you want to Slice in half, then slice again each half lengthwise into four strips. (Be careful! Sweet potatoes are difficult to cut, so just take it easy, and cut them thick). 2 reasons; it's easier to cut thick slices and plus they'll be juicer. There you have it! Smile.

OK now..............Coat a really big baking dish with olive oil (or just spray with Pam) and then pour remaining olive oil into a bowl. Plop all the sweet potatoes strips into the bowl and kind stir them around so they all get coated with the olive oil. If you need to...... get a pastry brush of some sort and spread the olive oil around on the sweet potatoes even better.
Now lay all the sweet potato slices on a baking dish of some sort – do not pile on top of each other.

Bake approximately 30 to 45 minutes.
Check after 30 minutes if not done enough for your liking, then bake another 10 or 15 minutes. Ovens vary, so keep that in mind.

After removing from oven, sprinkle with lime juice and serve.
Who knew Lime juice on Sweet Potatoes is Wonderful ? Try it!

ENJOY!

RECIPE FOR COMPASSION WHEN SOMEONE YOU KNOW LOSES A LOVED ONE TO DEATH

Have lots of compassion and patience for the person that loses their spouse or loved one because of Death. I can only imagine this is nothing like divorce or anything else. At least with divorce, you eventually cultivate feelings of dislike for the person that let you go or that you let go. With Death, you are forever in love with a person who is no longer here. Wow! Along with losing a child – this is horrible. Reach out to those people and pray for them. (Just another suggestion from Granny Nancy)

APPLE-LISCIOUS AKSPARAGUS

(I just wanted to spell it like that, it was fun.)

Pre-heat oven to 500

Ingredients:

Fresh Asparagus
Extra Virgin Olive Oil

Wash, drain and pat dry Asparagus.

Arrange on baking sheet cross ways.

Sprinkle with your favorite seasoning.
(I use Tony Chachere's Original Creole Seasoning)

(Although sometimes, when I am feeding someone who doesn't care for spice then I use, Lawry's Seasoning Salt)

ENJOY!

RECIPE TO BE OPEN TO LISTENING

Remember don't look at things as though someone is telling you what to do. It is better to look at it as though someone is showing you what to do.

FABULOUS FRESH GREEN BEANS

15 minutes

Actually, you could cook a massive amount of these and just make a meal out of it! They are so very good!

Ingredients:

A package from Sams or Costco, or even maybe another grocery store – but not frozen)

Olive Oil
Tony Cachere's Original Creole Seasoning (optional)
Lawry's
Salt Pepper
Garlic Powder

Wash. Rinse and pat dry green beans.
Put in large pot.
Drizzle olive oil over green beans.
With large spoon stir and get all green beans coated with the olive oil.

Season with each of the above seasonings by sprinkling cross ways over entire pot and stir.
Turn burner on medium and stir often, like ever 3 minutes or so. You will probably cook for a total of about 15 to 20 minutes.

Don't cook to death! Ok? We want them to taste fresh and not all limp.

ENJOY!

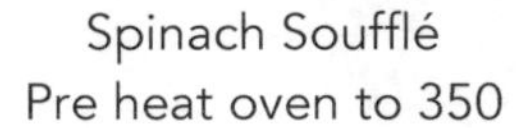

Spinach Soufflé

Pre heat oven to 350

4 packages frozen chopped spinach
1 8 oz. container of sour cream
1 large bag of shredded sharp cheddar cheese (you decide how much cheese you like. I like a lot!)
Salt and Pepper to taste
Chopped Water Chestnuts (optional)

Cook frozen spinach slightly (just enough to get it warm, do not overcook, as you will still be baking it too)
Drain spinach.
In large bowl stir in sour cream and shredded cheddar cheese to the spinach.

Lay in baking dish and top with more shredded cheddar.

Bake @ 350 for about 30 minutes.

Serve as a side dish.

ENJOY!

RECIPE TO UNDERSTANDING CHILDREN & FRIENDS OR NO FRIENDS

Do not over rate the need of your children having friends. As long as they are living at home it is better to spend the majority of your time doing things as a family. This way you can have more influence and control over what they are exposed to.
Not to mention, as adults we have learned that friends are few and far between. Don't teach your children to trust friends as it is better if they learn that people have to EARN your friendship over a long period of time. Right? Right.

SQUASH & ZUCCHINI

Big Hint:
Look for squash with no breaks, gashes or soft spots. Smaller squash (under 8 inches) are sweeter and have fever seeds; do not peel, just scrub off real good.

Cut squash lengthwise into ¼ inch strips,

Brush strips with olive oil.

Place in frying pan to sauté.

Have on medium heat.

Lightly brown.

ENJOY!

RECIPE ON TO TEACH YOURSELF TO NOT BE A "HATER"

All you haters out there...............

(I think I can help you get over your disorder of hating for no reason)Listen up..........(and ask yourself)Why do you have hatred for someone who has not personally impacted your life? That is simply unintelligent! Get a life and let others live theirs, they are not accountable to you. Think about what I have said and I'm sure you will now be able to put it in perspective. Stop hating, Think about that! Also, just as important it serves no purpose and is unhealthy.

BAKED SWEET POTATOES

PHAT TIP WHEN PURCHASING:
Look for paper skins with tapered ends.
Pre-heat oven to 500

Wash sweet potatoes.

Cut in ½ or whatever size you like. (keep in mind, the smaller the cut the faster they cook – you decide according to your schedule).

Brush on Olive oil and cook for 45 minutes.

After 45 minutes, check with a fork, if not real soft in the middle cook for another 45 minutes and check again, till they reach the desired softness that you like.

To keep them moist, drizzle more Olive oil on them after cooking.

Of course if you just want to go all out..........when time to serve:

Slather with butter and brown sugar.

If you just want to go crazy! After adding butter and brown sugar, drizzle with honey!

ACTUALLY, TO BE HONEST, THE BEAUTY OF COOKING SWEET POTATOES FOR SO LONG IS YOU DON'T EVEN REALLY NEED ANY BUTTER OR ANYTHING. ALWAYS REMEMBER TOO, THAT YOU CAN REPLACE BUTTER WITH OLIVE OIL. HMMMMMM GOOD!
ENJOY!!!!!!!!

SWEET POTATOES

Lisa Douglass

You will need a Crock Pot for this one

YAY! Easy. LOL

Ingredients:

Sweet Potatoes (NOT YAMS) Amount? You decide.

Wash sweet potatoes really good.

Stab each one with a fork several times -or- cut up in a smaller size.

Put 1 Tablespoon water in crock pot.

Put crock pot on HIGH

Cook for as long as you like, 4 to 5 hours is good.

Turn off crock Pot.

Remove and eat.

These will be cooked so well that you will not need any butter or anything else, just eat as they are.

ENJOY!

RECIPE ON BEING GRATEFUL

Always, Always, Always remember.................

God is the one who wakes you up everyday.

TURNIPS

PHAT TIP WHEN PURCHASING:

Look for smaller turnips with firm, white skins. They should feel heavy and the greens should still be attached.

Get out big skillet as you will need to sauté turnips.

Cut off the root end of the turnips, Peel the turnips and rinse real good.

Cut into match stick style.

To the pan add 1 teaspoon butter and 1 teaspoon olive oil, Turn heat to medium, and add turnips to the pan. Salt and pepper!

Begin to sauté till reaching desired tenderness.

Stay near pan and stir from time to time and you can put the lid on from time to time.

The main thing is; DO NOT LEAVE UNATTENDED as olive oil will begin to burn easily.

Once your turnips Have reached their desired tenderness, serve and ....

ENJOY!!!!!!!!

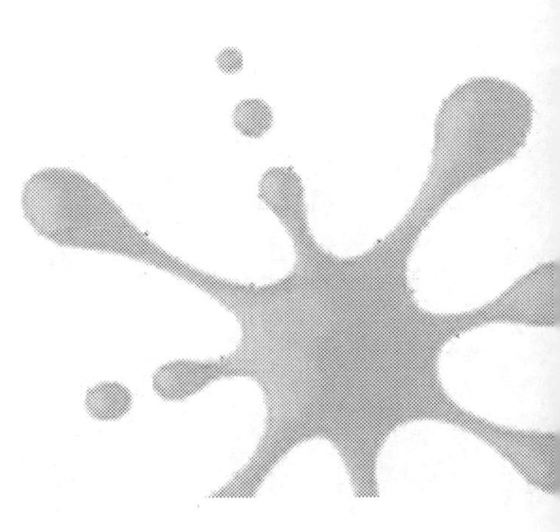

CHOICE RECIPE?

I choose................

To live by choice, not by chance;

To make changes, not excuses;

To be motivated, not manipulated;

to be useful, not used;

To excel, not compete;

I chose self esteem, not self pity;

I choose to listen to my inner voice; not the random opinions of others.

(Write that down somewhere, I loved! I have always wondered who wrote that?)

Here's a Great LOVING RECIPE

Are are you hating people that hate you? DON'T!

Use your time loving people who love you! Hellooooo! LOL

Sweet Corn
YIELDS 4 TO 6 SERVINGS

1 Pound frozen Corn
1 ½ cups (12 ounces) Whipping Cream
1 ½ tablespoons plus 1 tablespoon Butter (divided use)
1 ½ tablespoons all-purpose flour
2 tablespoons Sugar
1 teaspoon Salt
3 tablespoons grated Parmesan Cheese

Procedure:

- In a large pot, combine Corn and Whipping Cream and bring to a boil.
- Remove Corn from Cream with slotted spoon and set aside. Return pot of Cream to stove.
- In a small bowl, make a paste with 1 ½ tablespoons Butter and Flour. Gradually add to hot cream, and stir to combine and thicken.
- Reduce heat and simmer for 5 minutes. Add Sugar and Salt.
- Turn on oven broiler.
- Return Corn to Cream mixture and return to boil.
- Remove from stove, and pour creamed Corn into a 9-by-9 inch casserole dish.
- Top with Parmesan Cheese and dot with remaining tablespoon of Butter.
- Place casserole dish under broiler and brown.
- Serve hot.

ENJOY!

SWEET POTATOES WITH PINEAPPLE

Preheat oven 400 degrees

Ingredients you will need:

- 6 small sweet potatoes
- 1/3 as much pineapple as potato
- 1/3 cup of honey
- ¼ cup of water

Boil the potatoes with the skins on.

When cool, peel and cut them in pieces one-quarter of an inch thick.

Mix honey and hot water.

Just cover the bottom of a baking dish with the mixture, add the sweet potatoes and sliced pineapple.

Pour the remaining honey mixture over them and bake for ten minutes in the oven at 400 degrees.

ENJOY!

Remember this.........

The world suffers a lot, not because of the violence of bad people,

but......because of the silence of good people.

NAPOLEON

Modern Vegetable Medley

This can be an entire meal!

This is a common sense recipe in terms of amounts. If you have a lot of people use a lot of Veggies. If you are going to use a lot of veggies – use a big pot instead of a frying pan. Capishe? (me personally, I make a lot every time. It is a great dish to have a lot of left overs. Because left overs = lunch at work the next day or so)

Olive Oil
Butter (not margarine)
Zucchini (any color or squash of any kind)
Sliced Mushrooms
Red Onions – cut in strips
Worcestershire Sauce
Garlic Salt (or powder, you choice)
Black Pepper

Wash all your vegetables, slice and make sure they are good and dry.

Get large frying pan.
Add Olive Oil.
Turn your burner to Med high.
Add all your Veggies.
Sprinkle with Garlic Salt, Pepper and Worcestershire Sauce.
Saute, mix all together, put top on pan and sauté for about 5 minutes.
Don't overcook.
Stir and check it out, let your veggies have at a least a little crunch to them.
Oh, and if you like...... add a smidge of butter and stir around.

CONTINUED ON NEXT PAGE............

P.S. To make this dish more Hearty and filling, if you have any left over meat or chicken.....then chop it up and add it in at the end. (add it at the end so it doesn't get cooked and tough but yet it will get tossed around and get warm along with the veggies.

Everyone is going to love this!

Enjoy!

RECIPE ON UNDERSTANDING VENGEANCE

How about this:

Wise is the person who understands that the right to "vengeance" belongs to the Lord.

SIMPLE TRUTH and a recipe

Everyone that you meet comes with some baggage,

Find someone who loves you enough to help you unpack.

-or-

Unpack together?

How about that?!

Honey Roasted Carrots

3 to 4 bunches fresh Carrots, peeled
2 Tablespoons extra-virgin Olive Oil
2 tablespoons Honey
Salt
Ground Black Pepper to taste

Pre-heat oven to 450 degrees

- Steam your carrots before baking by placing them in a covered glass dish (only ½ teaspoon water); put them in the microwave on high for about 4 minutes or so. Capishe? (Translation....... Italian for Do you understand?)

- Ok, now..............Toss with the Olive oil, honey, salt, and pepper.

- Last of all, put all the Carrots on a shallow baking sheet in a single layer and bake for about 25 minutes or so.........to your own liking.

Loosen them from the baking sheet with a spatula and serve!

ENJOY!

GOT ANY MATERIALISTIC FRIENDS?
This recipe may help them.

Recipe to Realize Reality

If you think you are going to build self esteem from having lots of possessions, it is not true.
(That is called "Insanity")

Fresh Broccoli

Wash and put in glass baking dish with top with 1 Tablespoon water.
Grate a bit of lemon over top (optional)
Sprinkle with Olive oil.
Add Parmesan cheese (optional)
Salt
Pepper

Microwave on High for 4 minutes, do not remove top of baking dish for at least 2 minutes.

ENJOY!

In the wrong relationship?

Here's a suggestion:

You have got to get away from the wrong one to be able to find the right one.

Capishe????

Hellooooooooo!

Recipe to stop the heartache and to stop crying

Instead of wiping away your tears,
Wipe away the people who made you cry.

RECIPES TO BE HELPFUL TO PARENTS
OR YOU MAY CALL THEM OPINIONS LOL

Either way.......they are meant to be helpful in parents everyday life

Ok, Parents.......Lets' remember what may possibly happen if we fail to prepare our children for life. EXAMPLE: Think about this.......if you don't prepare them and they go out into the world to say...........get a job? And they are not prepared and in the interview are they going to say, sorry, my parents didn't prepare me, could you just consider me anyway? Yeah, right. They will most likely say, there's the door, NEXT! Now your grown child didn't get the job and now you have a stay at home grown child.

So here's the deal, every decision you make has an impact on your child. Whether you had no choice to make that decision or not ....there was still an impact! So when you have a choice as to decisions that effect your kids too, think them all the way through. In other words, don't just think of yourself and your own feelings. Capishe?

OH, AND ANOTHER THING......if you are at home and you have a FAMily ....

There should be no "multi-tasking". This is a new term everyone uses. On a personal level it often may not work. (meaning while at home - get off the phone during family hours) You are basically just switching from doing one thing to the next. So you really are not doing any one of them with any kind of intensity at all. Be present with everything you do. Our state of mind (attitude) is one of our most precious gifts that we give to one another. Address your state of mind first. Does that make sense?
If your child is in your presence, then that is where your focus should be. It's that simple.

WAIT, THERE IS STILL MORE.......

When having conversations with other parents of children that know your children, ...you must protect your child without betraying them.. Don't tell your children's business! (especially if people are already hating on you anyway, you will just give them ammunition) Just remember, who ever you talk to WILL repeat your conversation at some point to somebody! Like they used to say; don't tell the trees what you don't want the wind to know. (Fact: the wind blows where ever it pleases)

Teach your daughter self worth. So she won't think she needs a boy to like her to make her think she's worth something!

Parents; Quit making your agenda to suit yourself - that's making your agenda at the expense of your children. ....once you decided to have children your own agenda is secondary. Run an agenda that is in their best interest.

To those of you who believe your parents beat the crap out of you so you are going to do the same to your children? I am here to tell you: You cannot beat the personality out of your child! You cannot beat them into a whole new person. It is an endless battle and in the long run you just basically relieved your own anger. Come on! You slap their little hand and their little hiney a little here and there when they are young but at some point they understand you through verbal communication. Try it.

Young parents you must remember you must make rules for your children! You must have clear boundaries. And you have to enforce them. If not..........they will make their own rules. (they are not qualified to do so) Helloooooooooo, then you wonder why they are out of control?

Remember Mom's.........lets guide our daughters that have missing fathers very carefully. Some of these girls will possibly jump at the first guy that comes along and pays attention to them and tells them all the things we girls love to hear. So Mom's, lets educate our precious girls to not just react to what feels good. For starters, teach your girls to think for along time first as to why a guy would be telling her all these wonderful things if he doesn't even barely know her? Hmmmm?

My Family is my "Estate", I have accrued so much Equity. What a Blessing!
IS YOUR FAMILY YOUR ESTATE? (Think about it, THEY SHOULD BE)

Oh, and for all you women out there that had a bad experience or two....don't bash every man for it! Ok? There are a lot of good men out there, God made sure of that. Put your Trust in God. Without forgiveness you will never experience real love again! Remember that.

VARIOUS Big TIPS
ON LOVE AND DATING

If you have secured someone's heart do not abuse it!

Make your relationship what you want it to be:
You want affection - be affectionate
You want excitement - be exciting
You want respect - be respectful etc.......
IT'S THAT SIMPLE -You decide.

Every woman/man has the love life they want, it is that simple. We plan our own lives.

Ask yourself; Do You love that person? You know what their needs are? Meet their needs then!. It is that simple - that is what we do when we love someone. Need I go on?

MORE Big TIPS

DATING........I'm GOING TO BE BRUTAL.......Read on...............

Dating..........don't pursue someone you don't plan on loving - don't get into their heart if you don't have good intentions

If you are dating a loser - when it is over, don't be hurt, sad or discouraged. Hellloooooo - you lost a looser! This is great! It is over! Yay! (Be grateful)

Are you having confusion, doubt, are you hesitant, skeptical, distrustful, suspicious, apprehensive, and are you having uneasy feelings of a certain person in your life? Well............cut to the chase with yourself. If your family, brother, sister or friends knew everything (and that includes every little thing that you know) about this man/woman, would they like, accept and respect them? If your answer to yourself is no, then there! You have your answer to yourself........ move on! Your'e not dating for a sport are you?

Here's a good one: Don't use your body to have power. God Knows.

Do not tell a new person details about your last relationship if it was abusive in any type of way! Read on.........................

Do not tell a new person in your life about what you allowed that last person to do to you that you wish you could undo. Know what I'm saying? If you do, you will be sorry. Those of you that tell the story of an abusive previous relationship to someone new in your life, you are basically painting a picture that you have been mistreated and you allowed it. You may be asking for trouble again. You will basically be saying these are the things I accept or you want pity? So......it is simple: if you want change, make a change. We must learn from our mistakes. Remember the saying: Don't let anyone see your cards! Hellooooooo. LOL

Are you looking for a man or woman so you can have all the things you've always dreamed of? Perhaps a house, a new car, beautiful clothes, jewels?

Can't seem to find him? Do you think that is the right thing to do?

K'mon....Don't ask someone else to reach for <u>your</u> dreams. <u>You</u> reach for them! God knows what you're up to. (Again, always remember, God gets the news first) Don't get with someone because of what you can get. It is wrong, wrong, wrong. You know that.

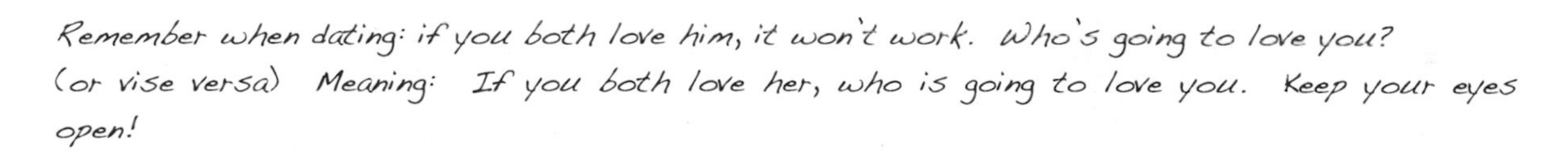

Remember when dating: if you both love him, it won't work. Who's going to love you? (or vise versa) Meaning: If you both love her, who is going to love you. Keep your eyes open!

When you have found your true love, you won't have to convince yourself to believe it. You will simply know it.

Dating when your over 40: You must be wise. You just cannot expose yourself to financial exploitation, especially after a certain age. You cannot afford to divide your wealth in half after a certain age. Financially the older you get the harder to replenish yourself monetarily. Your earning capacity diminishes and your needs for support and care increases. These are simple facts. You must protect yourself in every way. I always say when you are single nobody is looking out for <u>you</u> but <u>YOU</u>. So.........move forward with caution.

There is a time to know when a relationship is over, a time to move on, when you are no longer emotional about it....then perhaps that would be the best time. Don't quit with unfinished emotional business. Anger and hurt needs to be completely gone. It will be better that way. Just a thought.

Don't get involved with a Convict! Ever! They will con you every time. Convict = Con. Anyway that has served prison time, you must remember when they get out of jail- they are still the same person as they were previously! (They don't do make over's in prison, helloooo!)

Ask yourself, why pursue commitment when so many things about that relationship just aren't right? Let it go. If you feel like you are chasing or forcing it to fit - then you are. That's why God gave us instincts, intuition. It is a blessing to be able to have those feelings, it is an internal protection mechanism God blessed us with. Listen to yourself. (it is God speaking through you)

Recipe for Love

2 Knee's for Praying
4 Thighs
52 tablespoons Heaping Passion
1 cup Satisfaction
4 oz. of Sweetness
5 Kisses
2 soft Sighs
1 cup of Lasting Hugs
1 cup of Caring Words

Sprinkle in:

15 Gallons of Attraction
5 Gallons of Trust
5 Gallons of Respect
5 Gallons of Forgiveness
5 Gallons of Understanding
5 Gallons of Patience
5 Gallons of Giving of Self
5 Gallons of Appreciation
5 Gallons of Communication

Heat must be at boiling point.
Layer thighs and remaining ingredients.
Stir Lovingly with Firm stick.
Spread with Cream
Put in oven and repeat as often as needed
Serves 2

FAST THROW TOGETHER LITTLE MEALS

FOR

COLLEGE DORM

OR

EVEN ON THE ROAD LIKE FOR A MOTEL ROOM WHEN YOU'RE ON THE FLY

HEALTHY COLLEGE DORM ROOM DINNER

Inspired by:
My Grandaughter "Niko" -aka- College student
AT
Texas A & M

Ingredients you should have:

- Turkey Sausage (or chicken sausage – already cooked, see label)
- Avocados
- Black Beans (canned –drain)
- Green Onions (wash and chop)
- Tomatoes (wash and cut or dice)
- Sun-dried Tomatoes (in olive oil)
- Ritz Crackers (or the cracker of your choice)

Cut sausages and dump in pan with a little olive oil and brown (remember it is already cooked, you are basically just warming up) Actually, a little blackened is really good too.

Wash Avocado skin, cut open in half and then slice out. (you know....like you see them do at Subway Sandwich Shop)

Lay all ingredients out on a platter (or dinner plate)

Healthy! Easy! And Good!

ENJOY!

Never Fail Fudge
From Aunt Marge's Recipe book

Great for College students to make in the Dorm
No oven needed, just stove top

Things you will need:

Pam cooking spray to grease Pan
1 square baking pan about 8 inches
1 small/medium Pan

10 large Marshmallows
2 tablespoons water
2 cups of sugar
2/3 cup can Pet Milk (just buy 1 can)
1 cube Butter
1 small package Semi Sweet Chocolate Chips
1 teaspoon Vanilla extract or flavoring
Chopped walnuts (optional)

Melt together Marshmallows with 2 tablespoons water, 2 cups of sugar and 2/3 cups Pet milk, cook about 6 minutes stirring constantly. Now.............
Remove from heat, then add,,,,,,,,,,,,,,,,
1 cube of Butter
1 package Chocolate Chips
1 teaspoon Vanilla
Stir, stir and stir. Pour "immediately" into square 8inch pan and put in refrigerator for 2 hours.

Then cut in squares and...............
ENJOY!

THIS FUDGE GOES GREAT WITH HAWAIIAN PUNCH !

RECIPE TO FIGURE OUT HATERS

The People who hate you are just "your" confused admirers.
They can't figure out the reason why everyone else loves you.

LOL LOL

COLLEGE DORM EASY HEALTHY LUNCH
(or you can even pretend like this is dinner)

Ingredients you will need:

- Saltine Crackers (or your favorite cracker)
- Smoked Sardines
- Sun-dried Tomatoes in Olive Oil
- Hot Sauce (Optional)
- Applesauce (desert)

Get Platter (or dinner plate, or paper plate).
Arrange Crackers around the edges.
Open smoked Sardines, place in little small bowl in center.
Open Sun-dried Tomatoes, place in little small bowl, place in micro wave for 30 seconds.

Get your cracker, put some sun dried tomato on top, place a Sardine on top and sprinkle with Hot sauce!
WHA-LA!

ENJOY!

FOR DESSERT

Have some Applesauce!

It doesn't get any easier than that !!!!!!!!

RECIPE TO STEP UP YOUR OWN HAPPINESS
The following is the thought/analogy you must have.........

Trouble is inevitable at times
But....
Misery is optional.
(YOU KNOW THAT'S RIGHT!!!)

SALMON DIP and CRACKERS

1 package (8 ounces) Cream Cheese, softened
2 tablespoons chopped Onion
2 tablespoons Ketchup
1 tablespoon creamed Horseradish
1 can (7 ounces) Salmon, drained, and flaked (or canned shrimp)

- In a medium mixing bowl, blend cream cheese, onion, ketchup, and horseradish until well mixed.

- Fold in Salmon flakes and mix well.

- Serve with your favorite kind of Crackers!

ENJOY!

A THOUGHT
YOU CAN PRETTY MUCH EQUATE MATURITY WITH DEPENDABILITY......JUST A THOUGHT.
(if someone is immature then don't depend on them for anything)

VEGETABLE TRAY MICRO

Another great idea from Granny Nancy

BTW.....THIS IS ALSO GREAT FOR THE DORM

You know those trays of vegetables precut up for parties and what have you? Well..................Here's my big idea to make things simple – for a healthy meal.

By the Vegetable tray,

Trash the Ranch Dip (or save it for something else – your choice)

Dump all the Veggies in a big glass bowl.

Drizzle with Olive Oil.

Cover big glass bowl.

Place in microwave with a cover on top.

Cook on high for desired amount of time. I like to cook for 4 minutes, stir and sample and then microwave for another couple of minutes if needed.

Serve as an entire meal, (if you think just veggies isn't enough, then cut up some cooked sausage and throw in). Or, buy one of those already cooked chickens and have on the side. How about that?

ENJOY!

WATERMELON INFO

PER DR. OZ & DR. ROIZEN

Watermelon degunks arteries. Swapping watermelon juice for water reduces body fat, lowers LDL cholesterol and -the biggest effect- cleans heart-threatening plaque out of arteries. Early days on this research, but it fits.

Watermelon drops your blood pressure and boosts circulation. Watermelon is one of the few food sources of citrulline, a protein that's a real powerhouse. Got borderline hypertension? Citrulline lowers systolic blood pressure by as much as 9 points, enough to prevent full blown hypertension. That's because it helps produce nitric oxide, powerful stuff that opens and relaxes your arteries. Citrulline also turbocharges blood flow, enhancing circulation to all your vital parts. And Citrulline helps wound healing and cell division.

Watermelon is loaded with lycopene. This potent plant polyphenol is thought to fend off heart disease and some cancers. Cup for cup watermelon has 40 percent more lycopene than tomatoes.

Watermelon is naturally low-cal. There are only 96

calories in two cups of sweet watermelon. And you can buy 100 percent watermelon juice; if a health food store doesn't have it, Amazon.com does.

RECIPE TO REALIZE YOU CANNOT NOT CHANGE SOMEONE...

Do not date someone with the thought of changing them, as everybody that's grown is already who they are.

Well, let me say it like this......

Trying to change a grown man (or woman) would be like trying to eat applesauce with chopsticks.

Of course I guess there is the possibility of growing together?

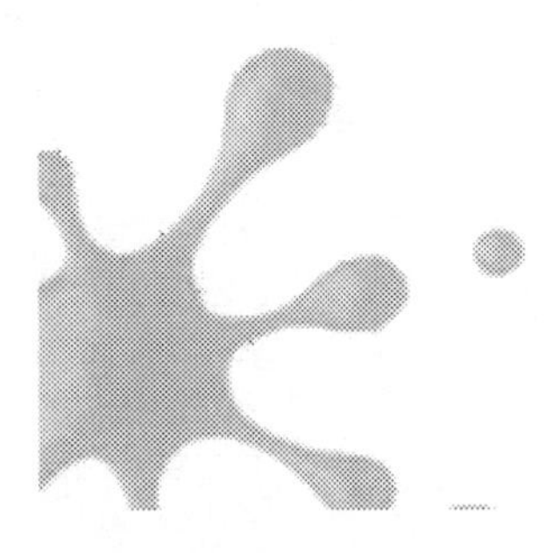

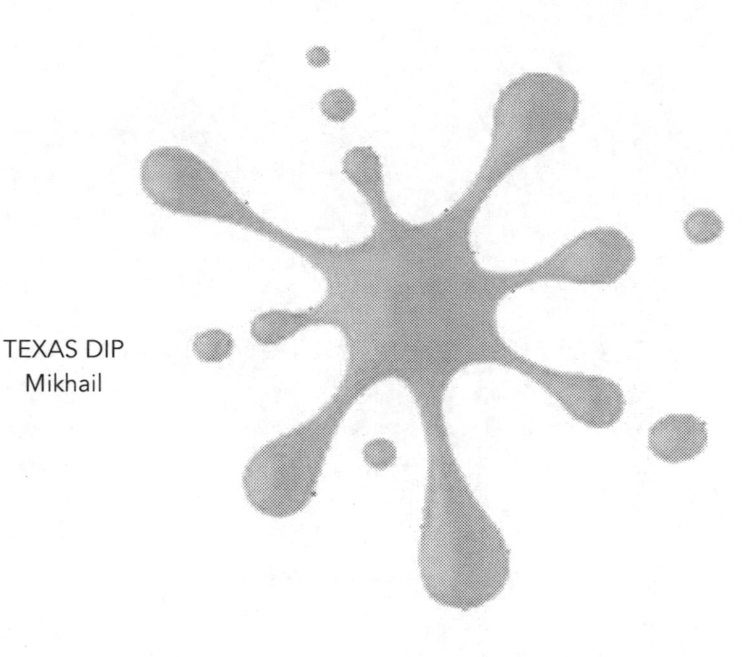

TEXAS DIP

Mikhail

2 cans Black-eyed Peas (Drained)
1 can Rotelle
Cilantro (wash and chop up)
Red Onion (peel and chop up)
Italian Vinaigrette Dressing

Mix all together and have some Tortilla Chips for Dipping.

This is a great filler upper.

ENJOY!

RECIPE ON LIFE

Life can only be understood backwards,
But must be lived forward.
Soren Kieregaard

RECIPE TO CONTROL ANTS !
CONTROL ANTS NATURALLY...

Get Ants out of your kitchen without using pesticides or bait traps: GO GREEN

Fact: "Ants follow chemical trails left by other ants to help them find food".

Follow the Ant's path backward to see where they get in. Use either: Coffee Grounds, Lemon Juice, Cinnamon, Cayenne Pepper or Citrus Oil to create a Barrier.

Good Luck! Get them Varmits out of there!

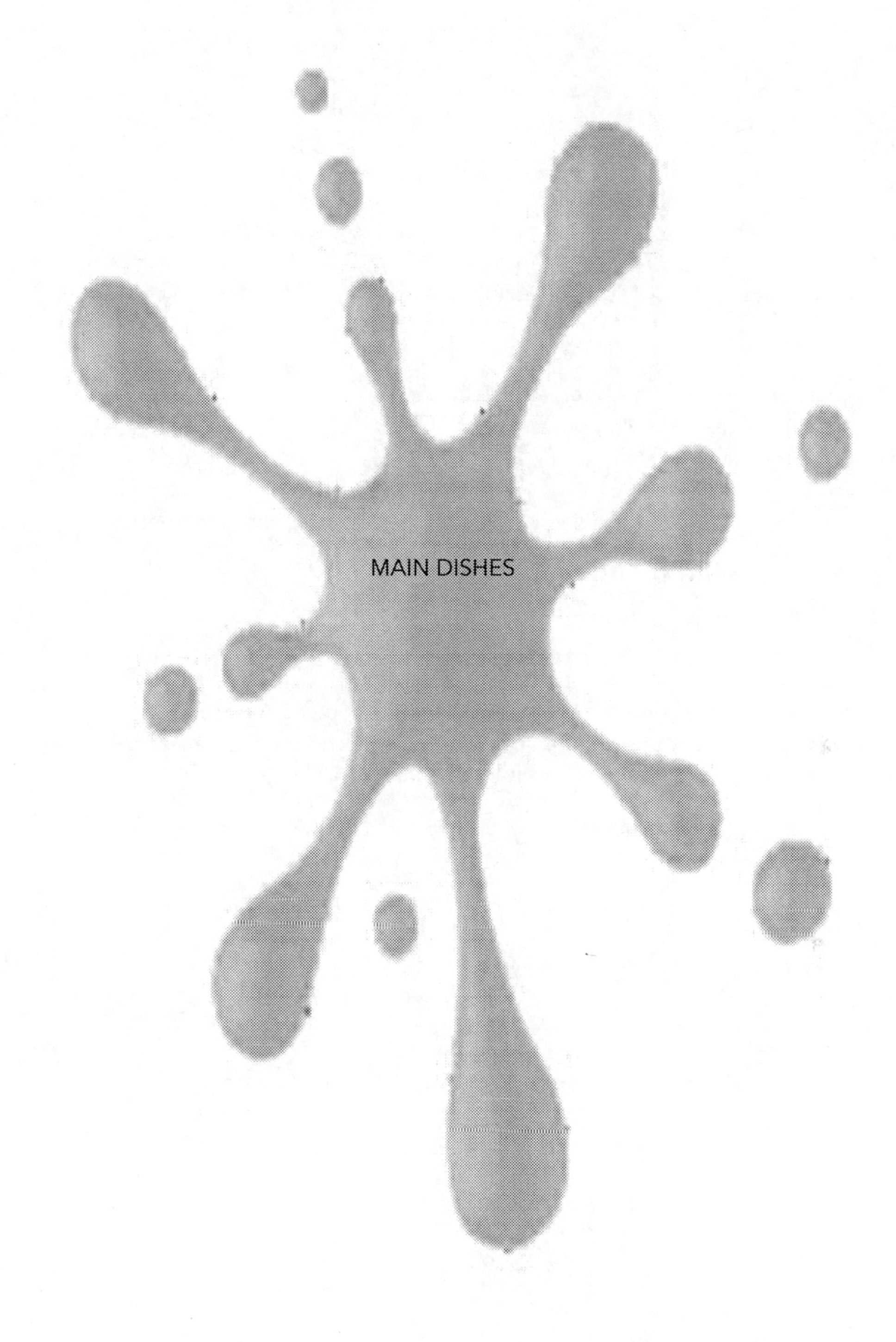
MAIN DISHES

Tomato Sauce – HOMEMADE

You will need a food processor

This is clean homemade sweet tomato sauce! It is Great!

1 large onion
8 fresh ripe tomatoes (or canned plum tomatoes, drained)
¼ cup good – quality extra-virgin olive oil
3 cloves garlic, minced

Chop onion in the food processor until finely minced. Coarsely chop the tomatoes in a food processor or blender.

Heat a medium skillet on medium heat.

Add olive oil.
when oil is hot, add minced onion and cook till translucent, about 4-5 minutes.
Add the garlic and cook for another minute, Add the coarsely chopped tomatoes and reduce heat.
Simmer for 45 minutes until sauce thickens a little.
.

ENJOY!

Preparing Chicken Safely

Raw chicken and other raw poultry can contain salmonella, the most common food-borne illness in our country. Please use the following handling procedures when working with raw poultry:
Cut raw poultry on nonporous plastic cutting boards. These cutting boards do not have the deep crevices that wooden ones have, where the salmonella bacteria can hide. For the same reason, do not use wooden utensils when cooking with raw poultry.

Be sure to wash cutting boards and knives with disposable paper towels, kitchen detergent and hot water before cutting anything else, so you do not contaminate other foods with the salmonella bacteria. Do not use sponges and washcloths because they, too, can contaminate kitchen surfaces and other foods with the salmonella bacteria. Be sure to cook boneless chicken breast to an internal temperature of 170 degrees and whole chicken to 180 degrees to kill the salmonella bacteria.

RECIPE TO BE FRIENDLY EVEN WHEN THEY ARE NOT YOUR FRIENDS

It is natural and simple to be friendly to friends. However, listen up! To be friendly to the enemy is most gracious. (of course always keep one eye open- like they say keep your enemy close so you stay informed, self protection too.) but be friendly and cordial.
(If needed, read the Paradoxical Commandments again)

Italian Chicken Pasta
Pre heat oven to 425 degrees

Ingredients:
8 ounces uncooked spaghetti
1 pound Asparagus, cut into 2-inch pieces
8 Sun–dried tomatoes , diced
2 cloves Garlic, finely chopped
1 ½ cups chopped yellow Bell pepper
¾ cup chopped red Onion
2 cups chicken Broth

1 ½ pounds or so (you decide) boneless, skinless Chicken breast halves, cut into ½ inch strips. (or cut how you like)
1/3 cup chopped fresh basil leaves
½ teaspoon salt
¼ teaspoon pepper
Once your oven is heated,
Cook your fresh skinless boneless Chicken breast at 425 degrees for 20 minutes. (after removing from oven cut thickest chicken breast in center and confirm there is no pink juice) It should be very tender.

Cook spaghetti as directed on package; drain. Set aside.
Cook asparagus, tomatoes, garlic, bell pepper and onion in broth in 10 inch skillet over medium heat. Cook 5 minutes.
Stir in cooked Chicken. Cook 2 to 3 minutes stirring constantly, until asparagus is crisp-tender. Stir in spaghetti and any remaining ingredients. Toss for a quick minute until heated. (I usually add a couple splashes of some flavored olive oil too). Salt and Pepper as desired and sprinkle your basil leaves also. (sometimes a sprinkle some Italian seasoning too.)

This will make about 6 servings. **ENJOY!**

CHICKEN "N" DUMPLINGS

JUST PLAIN GOOD EATIN'

OK, SO! I have tried while writing this book to provide simple, succulent, soul satisfying suggestions for good eating. I have included some recipes that are different and easy enough that even beginning cooks can follow them.

So one of everybody's cold weather dinners is Chicken and Dumplings, right?

Many people make a big chore out making dumplings when in reality it's so simple even a child could make them – with this recipe.

This is a really good one-dish meal and not much more is needed except maybe some good bread for sopping up the sauce. OH and maybe some white wine and a taste of dessert.

Serves about 6

Ingredients:

1 whole Chicken (have the butcher cut up for you or buy the pieces that <u>you</u> like best)

1 Onion
4 carrots, sliced
6 stalks of Celery, sliced
3 sprigs of Parsley
2 teaspoons of Salt
1 teaspoon pepper
4 tablespoons Butter
3 tablespoons cornstarch
¾ up Milk or Cream
1 cup of flour

Wash Chicken real good and place in large pot.
Wash and slice the Carrots, place in the large pot.
Wash and slice the Celery, add to the pot.
Peel and slice the Onion, add to the pot also.
Add enough water to cover everything.
Bring to a boil.
Cover and simmer for about an hour.
Taste the broth and add the salt if necessary.
Continue cooking until chicken is tender when tested with a fork.

Remove the chicken to a covered glass dish or casserole bowl, the main thing is cover it to keep it warm.

Skim as much of the fat off the broth as you can.
Melt the Butter and blend in the Cornstarch.
Gradually stir in the milk which you have mixed with enough broth to get it warm.
Add your Cornstarch Milk mixture slowly to the broth in your pot stirring constantly to keep it smooth.
Cook until it reaches the consistency desired – about like thick cream.

NOW ....to make the DUMPLINGS...................

Boil 2 cups of water and add 2 tablespoons of butter.
Stir in 1 cup of flour and 1 egg.
Cook until thick enough to drop from end of tablespoon.

Put spoonfuls of the dumpling dough over the surface of the thickened broth and simmer for about 5 minutes.

Arrange the Chicken on a hot serving platter and pour the sauce over it.
Arrange the Dumplings around the edge and sprinkle with Parsley.

If you want to add a little gourmet touch to your dumplings, you may add 1 teaspoon of parsley, chives, basil, oregano or thyme as you stir in the flour.

ANOTHER METHOD YOU MAY LIKE,
CHECK IT OUT............

Cook the Chicken the same as above.
When it's done, remove the Chicken from the bones.
Thicken the broth as above and return the Chicken meat to the sauce.
Add half a pound of mushrooms sautéed in butter and heat thru.
Serve along with the dumplings OR Serve the mixture over hot biscuits, toasted English muffins, or cornbread.

The main thing is..................
ENJOY!

Recipe to Recognize if someone wants to be in your life....

If someone wants to be a part of your life, they'll make an effort to be in it. So don't bother reserving a space in your heart for someone who doesn't make an effort to stay.

Anonymous

Loving Sweet Power Beans

1 Extra Large can Baked Beans (DO NOT DRAIN)
1 Regular size can Kidney Beans (DRAIN)
1 Regular size can Northern Beans (white beans) (DRAIN)
1 Regular can Butter Beans (DRAIN)
½ cup Brown Sugar
¼ cup Vinegar
1 Tablespoon Mustard
Sausage (optional)
(take some cooked sausage and brown it in some olive oil and add to the beans)

Put all in Crock Pot on Low for the day.

ENJOY!

RECIPE TO BE CAREFUL

Be very careful never to forget what you have seen the Lord do for you. Do not let these things escape from your mind as long you live! And be sure to pass them on to your children and grandchildren. (Deuteronomy 4:9)

BAR – B – Q SOUP

THIS RECIPE You know how sometimes you just want something that taste like Bar-B-Q...........?
Especially in the winter or especially when you just want to make a pot of something that will go a long ways..................
Check it out...................................

Ingredients:

2 bottles of Hickory Honey Barb-B-Q Sauce (your choice of Brand)
1 huge package of Boneless skinless thighs
1 Red Onion (sliced)
1 large large can of Baked Beans (get the ones with Brown Sugar)
1 package frozen Corn
3 large sticks of Celery (diced)

Put everything together in your crock pot on high and cook all day.
YOU ARE GOING TO LOVE THIS SOUP!

SERVE IN LARGE BOWLS AND ENJOY!

Recipe to understand not to ask others for your next dream?
ENJOY!

COMES FROM A REALLY REALLY GOOD SOUTHERN COOK
FROM PORT HUENEME
Get out your CROCK POT! YAY! EZ!

SALMONETTES
(Salmon Patties)

Ingredients you will need:

- A (14 oz) can of Salmon (or Tuna)
- ¼ cup liquid from the Salmon or Tuna
- 1 egg, lightly beaten
- ½ cup flour
- 1 heaping teaspoon baking powder

Fill a deep fryer or skillet half-full of oil.

Preheat this while you are mixing the Salmonettes.

Drain all but ¼ cup liquid off of the canned fish and set it aside.

Put the Salmon or Tuna in a mixing bowl and break it apart with a fork until you have no big flakes.

Add the flour and egg.

You can add a dash of Pepper if you like, but NO extra salt.

Blend with a spoon until all of the flour is mixed in, but don't over-mix.

Add the baking powder to the liquid that was set aside and beat with a fork or whisk until frothy.

Immediately pour this into the fish mixture and stir until well blended.

It is important not to let the baking-powder mixture sit after mixing.

Pour it into the fish immediately.

Drop the mixture by spoonfuls carefully into the hot oil.
They will brown very quickly, so watch then closely.
Lift them out with a slotted spoon and drain on a paper towel.
You must cook this right away – it cannot sit.

Serve and **ENJOY!**

RECIPE TO BE HELPFUL RATHER THAN BOSSY

Don't just tell somebody what to do............

Show them how. (its all about the delivery)smile too.

Recipe on love and good works

Food for Thought

Many people are lonely because they build walls instead of bridges......."Let us consider one another in order to stir up love and good works".

-Hebrews 10:24

(Technically, let us outdo each other in being helpful and kind to each other and in doing good)

Pay attention everyone! Men and Women!

More free info for you to be aware of............

Know how to identify when someone is spending money on you because they like you, and they want to and it is coming from their heart - rather than someone who is investing in you because they have a motive that you don't know about. We don't want to fool ourselves but for our own protection we must be aware that it can happen to anybody. Gold-diggers come in all genders, ages, etc etc.

Also, know this: you don't have to be rich for them to latch on to you. Some of them just want to get a "free ride" even if all they get is a free place to stay, maybe free eatin, $20, $30$40 bucks here and there............helloooooooo Gold-diggers come in all styles, ranges, ages.

Just sayin..............................

AUTHENTIC PORK BURRITO
ETM
(EASY TO MAKE)

Judy Johnson who has been my dear friend since 1979 showed me this recipe. Everything Judy does and says is from her heart! They don't make them like her anymore! Kisses to Judy!

INGREDIENTS YOU WILL NEED:

- Flour Tortilla's
- Pork (either cook yourself or buy pulled pork if in a hurry)
- Red Potatoes
- Diced Ortega Chile's (don't drain)
- Cheddar Cheese
- Hot Sauce (optional)

Of course there can be many variations of this Burrito, If need be, you can use chopped up steak, ground beef, or chicken. What ever you please!

Saute your meat in some olive oil.
Cut your Red Potatoes very small and sauté till tender in separate pan.
Once meat and Potatoes are done, transfer to same pan.
Dump can of Ortega Chile's in with Meat and Potatoes.
Heat Tortilla over fire on gas stove – or – nuke in micro wave 30 seconds.
Lay out tortilla, add meat and potato and chile mixture.
Sprinkle cheese over top and roll up.

Wha-La! Of course Hot Sauce will make this a BIG HIT hit!!!!!!
ENJOY!

BIG BIRD SPECIAL

(Yields 4 servings)

***This is a special dish for those that say they don't eat Sushi as well as people who love Sushi. Big Bird loves this recipe LOL

You will need 1 Deep Fryer
Large bottle Vegetable Oil
2 cups of Long Grain Rice (cooked)
1 Bottle of Teriyaki sauce (thick)
1 pound fresh Scallops
½ pound fresh Salmon
1 large Zucchini
¾ cup Green Onions
2 cups Broccoli Florets
2 Avocados

- For starters, cook your rice as directed on package and cover to keep warm. Set aside.
- Plug in Deep Fryer and add Vegetable oil to begin heating to 400 degrees.
- Cut all ingredients to about the same size. (Which would be about 1 inch in size)? (Although I like to cut the zucchini in strips (like little tiny matches that come in a little box) just because I like to have one item with a different cut)
- Cut your avocado in slices.
-

Once Deep fryer indicates Oil is ready..........................
Scoop large scoop of rice onto each plate with ice cream scooper to make a nice round mound
Add Scallops, Salmon, Broccoli Florets, Zucchini and ½ of the green onions to the deep fryer basket and deep fry for about 3 minutes.
Pull basket up and let oil drain off.
Spoon over mound of rice.
Drizzle Teriyaki Sauce over the top
Add slices of Avocado to side of plate

ENJOY!

CHICKEN SAUSAGE WITH ROASTED POTATOES AND VEGGIES

Preheat oven to 450

Ingredients you will need:

1 package cooked spicy chicken sausage
1 pound small fingerling or red potatoes
1 yellow onion
1 cup baby carrots
1 red bell pepper
2 1/2 tablespoons olive oil
2 tablespoons minced fresh rosemary leaves or 1 tablespoon ground rosemary
4 cloves chopped garlic
1/4 teaspoon crushed up red pepper flakes
Sea Salt

Cut up sausage.
Cut potatoes into quarters.
Peel the onion and cut up.
Wash red pepper and dice. (not to small but kind of small)

Put sausage, carrots, bell pepper, onion and potatoes in a large roasting pan. Do not crowd.
Mix together Olive oil, red pepper flakes, garlic and rosemary – stir together to coat all with olive oil, add black pepper and mix together even more.
Put in oven for about 30 minutes, stirring a couple of times until you notice the potatoes are tender.

When done, take out of oven and drizzle with a bit more olive oil if necessary and season with Sea salt.

ENJOY!

AN IMPORTANT THOUGHT TO ALWAYS REMEMBER

Good relationships feel good, they don't hurt.

FOOD FOR THOUGHT
(great to know when raising children)

One must have the right of choice, even to choose wrong if he is ever to learn to choose right.

BY: Josiah C. Wedgewood

A GOOD RECIPE TO START YOUR DAY

When you wake up each day, ask yourself;
What might I learn today?

CRABMEAT SOUFFLE
4 TO 6 SERVINGS

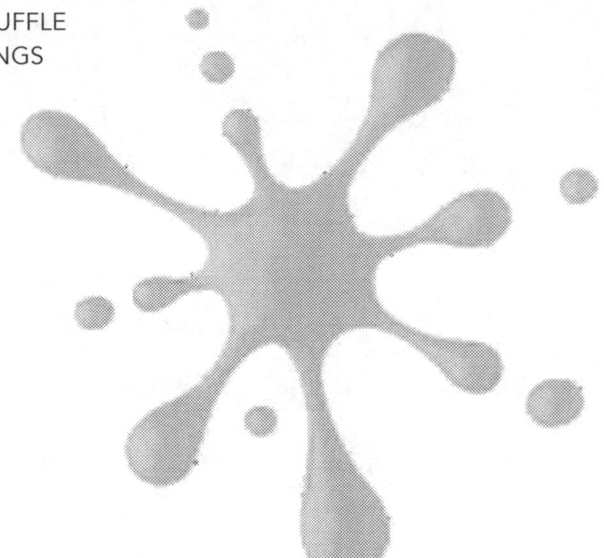

PREHEAT OVEN TO 300 DEGREES

Ingredients you will need:

- ½ cup (6 ½ oz can) flaked crabmeat
- ¼ cup butter
- ¼ cup flour
- 1 cup milk
- ½ teaspoon salt
- ¼ teaspoon curry powder
- 1 cup shredded Sharp Cheddar Cheese
- 4 eggs, separated

Place crabmeat in bottom of a 1 ½ quart soufflé dish.
Make a cream sauce with butter, flour, milk and seasonings.
Add cheese; stir until melted.
Remove from heat.
Gradually add slightly beaten egg yolks; cool.
Fold into stiffly beaten egg whites; pour over crabmeat in soufflé dish.
With tip of teaspoon, make slight indentation or "track" around top of soufflé 1 inch in from edge to form a top hat.

Bake at 300, 60 TO 65 MINUTES.

Serve immediately.

ENJOY!

Fried Catfish

Here's a great idea........

Take your Fryer on the patio so you don't smell up your house. (~_~)

Things you will need:

1 Deep Fryer (heat to 400 degrees)
1 pound Catfish (you can just keep frying batch after batch)
1 Large bottle of Vegetable oil
1 package all purpose flour
1 Box Yellow Cornmeal
Garlic Powder
Paprika
Black Pepper
Salt
*Seasoning Salt (I love Tony Cachere's & Lawrys) Use one of these for your last little sprinkle after fish is all fried up!

This is how you make it finger licking good!!

Plug in Deep fryer and add Vegetable Oil to designated line.

- Wash fish in Salt, Water, and squeeze lots of fresh lemon in there too. Drain. Pat dry with paper towel.
- Place on cutting board and season both sides with garlic powder, salt, and black pepper.
- Pour 3 cups cornmeal and 1 cup of flour in container.
- Season flour with Paprika.
- Roll fish in flour.
- Grab fish with Tongs, tap excess flour off, and place in Deep fryer basket.
- Make sure oil light signal is ready.
- Depending on size of pieces, add to deep fryer basket but do not crowd.
- Lower basket into cooking oil and cook. Amount of time to cook will depend on size. Remember my tips for Frying:

Granny's <u>Frying</u> Tips:

- TIP #1 once you no longer hear the fish sizzling...... this could be one indication that batch is possibly done frying.

- TIP #2 once your fish pieces are floating,.... This is another indication that batch is possibly done frying.

Once you remove your fish from the deep fryer, place it in a mesh strainer of some sort so any excess oil can drain off.

Right away, one last sprinkle with your choice of Seasoning, like Tony Cachere's and/or Lawry's.

ENJOY!

GREAT FACT FOR HATERS TO KNOW

Blowing out the other persons candle
Won't make your's shine any brighter.

By: unknown

RECAP RECIPE on "SECRETS"

Same recipe I have shared earlier in this book,
I just want you to remember this one......

If you reveal your secrets to the wind,
You should not blame the wind for blowing your secrets around.
By: Anonymous

SO DON'T BE GOING AROUND TELLING OTHERS ANYTHING.

Oh and just to close the deal.......
A gossip goes around spreading rumors, while a trustworthy man tries to quiet them.
(Proverbs 11;13)

Fried Chicken

1 Deep Fryer (heat to 400 degrees)
(I love the one I got on ebay brand new! Presto Fried Deep Fryer for $37.11, free shipping too)

1 Fryer Chicken –or- package of your choice, wings, legs, or thighs
(i cook a lot of wings these days since we have discovered fried food are not good for us. So at least wings are little, capishe?)

1 Large bottle of Vegetable oil
1 package all purpose flour
Garlic Powder
Paprika
Black Pepper
Salt
*Seasoning Salt (My favorite is Lawry's or when I feel like a little kick I choose Tony Cachere's – perhaps for your last little sprinkle <u>after</u> frying)

Plug in Deep fryer and add Vegetable Oil to designated line.

- Wash chicken real good with Salt and Water, Drain.
- While draining.......I spread out handy wrap over a large area on the counter top to lay my chicken out and I season Chicken real good on both sides and then when I'm done.......I just wrap it all up and throw away. Easy clean up, huh?
- Pour about 5 cups or more of Flour in container.
- Season flour with Paprika.
- Roll chicken in flour.
- Grab chicken with Tongs, tap excess flour off, and place in Deep fryer basket.
- Make sure oil light signals ready.
- Add about 4 or 5 pieces of chicken to deep fryer basket (do not crowd).
- Lower basket into cooking oil and cook for approx. 10 to 15 minutes (depending on size of chicken)

- TIP #1 once you no longer hear the chicken sizzling...... this could be one indication that batch is possibly done frying.

- TIP #2 once your chicken pieces are floating this is another indication that batch is possibly done frying.

Once you remove your chicken from the deep fryer, place it in a mesh strainer of some sort so any excess oil can drain off the chicken.

Right away, one last sprinkle with your choice of Seasoning.
(Lawry's seasoning salt is great for that last sprinkle!)

ENJOY!

Fried Chicken that's not Fried
From Lillian La Bahn

The secret to this recipe:
It is imperative to make sure the Chicken and the Yogurt are very, very cold.

Preheat oven to 400 degrees

Ingredients:
Light vegetable oil cooking spray
6 whole Chicken breasts, halved and skin removed
3 thighs, skin removed
3 ½ cups ice water
1 cup plain nonfat yogurt

Dry ingredients:

1 cup dried Italian Bread Crumbs
1 cup all purpose flour
1 tablespoon Old Bay seasoning
½ teaspoon Garlic Powder
½ teaspoon Creole Seasoning
1/8 teaspoon freshly ground black Pepper
½ teaspoon dried thyme
½ teaspoon dried basil
½ teaspoon dried oregano

Spray baking dishes with vegetable oil.
Have your chicken already in a bowl of ice cold water.
Have your Yogurt in another bowl on the side too.

Now, put all the breading ingredients into a large plastic zip lock plastic bag and shake real good.

Begin to put each piece of the chicken into the yogurt, then put in the bag and coat real good and lay in the baking dish.
Spray each piece of Chicken with the Vegetable oil.

Bake on the bottom shelf of the oven and bake for "about" an hour. (Key words: bake for about an hour? Various ovens are so so different, so it may be only 30 minutes!
After 30 minutes, turn the chicken and cut the center to determine how much more time to bake. (no pink juices should show on chicken) It may only need 15 more minutes as you don't want to dry it out. But I don't know every oven, so you will need to make an executive decision. Capishe?

ENJOY!

Fun Hot Dogs for Kids
On the Grill
Or
The Broiler

Cut ends in 4's about 1 ½ inches down (long ways), then Grill.
(this method will cause the hot dogs to curl up and kids love that!)

Tell the kids these are Octopus hot dogs.

Hmmmmmmm……a thought…..?

Sometimes Bad People are not really Bad,. They're just afraid.

(SO, give people a break sometimes already) Capishe?

Simple Bow Tie Pasta Dish

Stuff you will need:

Bow Tie Pasta
Chicken Strips (you can buy or make your own or see below)
Butter
Olive Oil
Peas (canned or frozen works)
Mushrooms (Sliced is better)
Garlic Powder

The Chicken: You could make Chicken strips out of Chicken Breast that you baked and then cut into strips.

OR

You can buy pre-made Chicken strips in the Deli section of the store where they sell the sammich (LOL) meat.

OR

You could purchase an entire already cooked Chicken at the store and just tear off the parts you want for your Pasta dish and save the rest of the Chicken for another recipe that calls for Chicken.

*Boil your Bow Tie Pasta according to directions on the package. Once cooked, drain.

*You should have your peas heating up on the side.....after heated, be sure to drain.

*Saute your sliced Mushrooms in Olive Oil, Butter and Garlic Powder really good.

Now..............TOSS everything together and serve.

ENJOY!

REAL FAST JUMBO LY-YA WITH A TWIST

Pre-heat oven to 435

10 Skinless Chicken Thighs
1 ½ Lb of Cooked Large Shrimp
1 Package Cooked Andoule Chicken Sausage (This is even better with Hot Links) just sayin.
Olive Oil
3 Celery Stalks (Chopped medium size pieces)
1 Green Pepper (Chopped medium size pieces)
1 Bunch of Green Onions (chopped)
1 Large Garlic Clove (diced)
Fresh Thyme (about 3 Tablespoons chopped up)
4 Tomatoes (cut in quarters)
2 Large cans Stewed Tomatoes
2 cans Chicken Broth (Just in case you need to make a little soupier)
½ cup Bar-B-Q Sauce
Creole Seasoning
Cayenne or Red Pepper (to your taste)
½ Teaspoon Garlic Powder
Black Pepper (to your taste)
Steamed Rice SEE "ALL ABOUT RICE" NEXT PAGE.....................

(Rice is great in a bowl under your Jumbo – Ly-ya or of course you can always eat the Jumbo Ly-ya as a soup – your choice!)

- Wash Chicken Thighs and drain in colander.
- Lay Chicken thighs out and season both sides with Garlic powder and Pepper.
- Arrange Thighs in large baking dish and put in oven for about 30 minutes.
- After Chicken has cooked, take out of oven, set aside.
- Cook Rice according to directions and set aside covered.
- Wash Shrimp and drain in colander and set to the side. (This will be the last thing you will add to this dish, remember these are already cooked – so you are simply re-heating them. Ok? Ok.
- Now............wash and chop the following ingredients; celery, green pepper, green onions, thyme, and tomatoes.
- Cut up Sausage.
- Take all of these ingredients and sauté lightly in pan with Olive Oil, a little garlic powder, a little pepper . (Do not over cook) Save this pan and the juices in it and after removing everything, throw your Shrimp in there with a little olive oil and diced up garlic and sauté for about 3 minutes.
- Ok.............Open your stewed Tomatoes and pour in large Pot. Cut heat on to about medium.
- CONTINUED ON NEXT PAGE..

- Add Sausage, celery, green peppers, green onions, thyme, and tomatoes to the stewed tomatoes.
- Ok, now for your Chicken, it should be falling off the bone – if not, no big deal as it will fall off once you add to your big pot of everything else. So....add your Chicken and Shrimp to the pot. (no need to cut up)
- Optional: Your personal choice, if you like your Jumbo-Laya to be soupier and go further add some Chicken Broth one can at a time. (Remember you can always add more but ya can't take out what you already poured in....so be smart add a little at a time till it's just like you want it, ok? Ok.

Now Season to your own liking with the Creole Seasoning and Red Pepper.

Get a big bowl, scoop some rice up, get a big fat spoon and pour the Jumbo-Laya over the rice.
ENJOY!

ALL ABOUT RICE

When a recipe calls for cooked rice, keep in mind these proportions: 1 cup of rice (cooked in 2 cups of water) yields about 3 cups cooked rice. Follow package directions, or here's a general guide: Measure water into a saucepan; bring to a full boil. Slowly add rice and return to boiling. Cover; simmer for time specified on package or until rice is tender and most o the water is absorbed. Remove from heat and let stand, covered, about 5 minutes.

JEVON DOUGLASS ONCE SAID.....

IF YOUR PRESENCE CAN'T ADD VALUE YOUR ABSENCE WILL MAKE NO DIFFERENCE.

RECIPE OF BEING A GOOD FRIEND

Well, this is just a little bit of that recipe as it takes even more than this. Just sayin................

Remember this; please......

As much as we might like to, we can't run our friend's life or use a personal yardstick to measure what is important to them. Maybe our friend has self esteem issues going on or something else, we sometimes just do not know everything about even our closest friends. The best thing we can do for someone we love is to pray for them. Most importantly of all, to remain a good friend, don't judge.

WE don't get to decide God's will.

Just sharing !!!

SWEDISH RICE PUDDING

Heat oven to 350

Get out casserole dish/bowl of some sort. (Grease it and set aside)

4 cups Milk
½ cup uncooked long-grain Rice
½ teaspoon Salt
4 Egg yolks
½ cup Sugar
2 tablespoons Butter, softened
1 teaspoon Vanilla
4 Egg whites
3 tablespoons Sugar

In a large saucepan, bring Milk to boiling. (don't let milk foam)
Stir in Rice and Salt.
Then reduce heat to medium-low.
Cook rice, uncovered for about 18 minutes, stirring a often.

In a medium mixing bowl, combine egg yolks, the ½ cup Sugar,
the Butter, and the Vanilla.
Beat until combined but not foamy.
Stir 1 cup of the hot Rice mixture into the Egg mixture.
While still stirring, pour all of the egg-rice mixture into rice mixture in the saucepan.
Bring mixture to boiling stirring constantly.
Cook and stir 1 more minute to thickened.
Now, pour pudding mixture into your prepared casserole glass bowl.
Meanwhile, in large mixing bowl beat Egg whites with electric mixer on medium speed for about 1 minute or until soft peaks form.
Gradually add the 3 tablespoons of sugar, 1 tablespoon at a time.
Beating on high speed for about 4 minutes or more forms stiff, glossy peaks form and sugar is completely dissolved.
Immediately spread the egg white meringue over rice pudding mixture, carefully sealing to the edge of the rice pudding.
Bake in a 350 degree oven for 15 minutes or until meringue edges are golden.

Serve warm or cold.

ENJOY!

PART OF AN OLD RECIPE

How kids used to grow up....

If u were raised on fried bologna, drank soda water, tasted powdered milk, played in the dirt, got whoopin's or got your butt spanked, had only "3" TV channels, changed a channel with a pair of pliers, began class with the "Pledge", had school clothes and play clothes, rode in the back of pick up trucks, played in the ditch, rode bikes without a helmut, recorded songs from the radio by blocking the holes on cassette tapes, drank water from a hose, and knew what time it was when the street lights came on and you still u turned out OK,,,,,,,continue to count your blessings. Just sayin.........

OH! And we didn't even call ANY adults by their first name!

Who started that crap anyway? LOL

Lemon Roasted Potatoes

Preheat oven to 425 degrees

2 pounds small red potatoes, washed and quartered
1 medium lemon, halved and sliced
1 tablespoon Olive Oil
2 teaspoons mince fresh Rosemary
½ teaspoon salt
1/8 teaspoon Pepper

Procedure:

Combine all ingredients in large bowl.
Toss around in bowl with large spoon and make sure each an every potato is coated with Olive oil.

Arrange in 12 X 10 inch baking pan coated with nonstick cooking spray.

Bake 35-45 minutes or until potatoes are golden and tender.

ENJOY!

RECIPE TO SAY WHAT YOU WANT to say:

WRITE YOUR OWN BOOK, then you can say anything you like.
THERE IT IS~ LOL

SO NOW I WILL WRITE WHAT I WANT TO WRITE THE MOST.........

IF HEAVEN HAD A PHONE......
I WOULD CALL MY Mom and Dad

Miracle Lemon Chicken

Preheat oven to 400 degrees

1 Whole Chicken (about a 4 or 5 pounder)
1 fresh Lemon
Garlic Salt
Oregano

- First things first.......Wash sink real well.
- Wash Chicken well! Rinse it, toss salt all over it and rub it around then rinse it off and set it in colander. Blaaa-Dow! It is clean!
- Now.....be sure to wash your hands real good and then go ahead and wash out your sink again because you don't want anything left of raw Chicken around!

How to Prepare!

- Place whole Chicken in a baking dish/pan.
- Squeeze Lemon all over Chicken and that put what's left of the Lemon in the inside of the Chicken.
- Sprinkle with Garlic Salt and Oregano to taste.

Bake at 400 for about35 minutes – cut into thickest part of Chicken and make sure no juices are pink. (If juices still pink, you must cook for a little longer) When done.....................

ENJOY!

ANOTHER GOOD RECIPE FOR

DAILY HAPPINESS

When you are thinking of your life........................
When you are getting your thoughts in order......
When you are just generally thinking ....

AGAIN...............Only count the good things, do not count the bad!

(By the way....... God is the "original" positive thinker..... "This [is] the day [which] the LORD hath made; we will rejoice and be glad in it." ~ Psalm 118:24)
Again, just saying.............

POTATO SOUFFLE

Preheat oven to 375 degrees

Ingredients you will need:

- ¼ cup grated mozzarella cheese
- 1 pound white potatoes, peeled
- 3 tablespoons butter
- ¼ teaspoon nutmeg
- ½ cup light cream, heated
- 4 egg yolks, room temperature
- 6 egg whites, room temperature,
- Salt & Pepper
- Dash paprika
- Dash savory
- Dash cayenne pepper
- Extra butter for mold

Prepare 6- cup soufflé mold by greasing well with butter and sprinkling sides and bottom with mozzarella cheese; set aside.

Cut potatoes into small pieces to decrease cooking time and place in saucepan filled with water; season with salt.

Boil until just cooked – do not overcook!

Puree through potato ricer or food mill into large bowl.

Stir in butter until well incorporated. Add all seasonings and mix well. Pour in cream and incorporate. Mixture should have consistency of mashed potatoes. Continued on next page……
Using wooden spoon, beat in all egg yolks at the same time. Set bowl aside.

Beat egg whites until stiff, using copper bowl if available, and spoon a bit of white into egg yolk mixture. . Incorporate well.

Fold egg yolk mixture into egg whites, using rubber spatula to incorporate evenly. Rotate bowl while folding and continue until no trace of white is left.

Pour batter into mold and run thumb around inside edge, about ½ inch deep into batter. This will form an extra little top.

Bake 35 minutes **ENJOY!**

RECIPE TO SEE FRIENDSHIPS AS THEY ARE

Don't fool yourself ON FRIENDSHIPS..................

Friendships sometimes end for one reason or another. They just do. Later in life I have learned to see it as it is. I can tell you about it now and you can have one eye open. There seems to be no purpose in working on repairing a relationship that was more one sided in the first place.

Breakdowns in relationships can fall into 3 types........... (again, my opinion)

1st....., there is the "Falling out of touch". Nobody's fault really. That is no one's malicious intention. Life sometimes sets people on different paths and we fall out of touch with one another. Once you notice, you can either let it go or you can renew your friendship. Or sometimes a friendship has been cultivated so that you can fall out of touch and reconnect months or even years later and then just pick up where you left off. It's all good. (from my point of view, that is a great friendship to have. One where there is no blame, heck! No reason for blame, that's life. No need to turn it into something negative.

2nd.......Then there is "The Injustice/Wrong/Insulting" relationship/friendship. (or former friendship now, lol) This is when you have a legitimate claim on the neglectful, disrespectful or in some cases outright ugly behavior of someone from whom you deserve better. Depending on how important the relationship is to you, the person that was ugly should begin a dialogue of reconciliation with apologies of some sort or at the least attempts to undue what they said/ clean up what they said or did and <u>if none of these takes place.</u>.....that person clearly "said" or did what they did to end the friendship as they had no courage to end it any other way but by being ugly. For me I simply end the relationship by falling off the face of the earth so to speak, I am now unreachable by phone, email, mail or facebook. If you think back the friendship probably only existed for their benefit anyway, right? The End for that one, that person decided they didn't want your friendship. I can accept that., because now I really don't care to continue the friendship now that they confirmed who they really are.

3rd.......is Disloyalty/Deception/Stab in the back......... Now this is a tough one too! Certainly for me. Basically, throw me under the bus for the purpose of political gain or because you are a political coward or simply because of spite....or for me, if you insult or hurt my husband, daughters or grandchildren......now you have permanently changed my ability to ever completely trust you again.....and in some severe cases to ever even speak to you again. Disloyalty and deception leaves me terribly disappointed. Wondering how a relationship that I once enjoyed and thought was close, supporting and loving could have possibly come to this? Perhaps now you have doubt as to whether the relationship was ever as close, supportive and loving as it appeared to be.? Probably not. (However I will continue to pray for you)

You have to move forward, you may be moving forward with a sense of loss. So we have sadness, anguish and just an obvious sense of suffering but we recognize and move on, we get past it......but we live and we learn and pray. Remember there is an endless supply of people in the world. So we meet new people, make new friends and it is all good.

We learn from life experience. The main thing is we don't let anything change our Hearts. Capishe?

Really Really Fast Veggie Lasagne

Or, hey a quick dinner to throw together in 10 minutes for any non -red meat eating hungry person!

Preheat oven to 350 degrees

Large package of Veggie Burgers
Lasagne rolled flat like homemade (no boiling required)
3 cans of Tomato Sauce
Bag of Baby Spinach
Shredded cheese optional – or if you're a cheese lover throw over each layer!
Garlic Powder
Pepper
Italian Seasoning
Large flat baking dish

(if you don't have Italian seasoning for your tomato sauce, then just use a jar or can of spaghetti sauce or pizza sauce instead of tomato sauce)

Take your veggie burger patties and line bottom of pan.
Pour tomato sauce generously over veggie patties and smooth over with back of a spoon.
Sprinkle lightly with Garlic powder, black pepper, and Italian seasoning.
Sprinkle layer of cheese
Layer 1 layer Lasagne over veggie burgers.
Pour tomato sauce again and spread over lasagna noodles.
Sprinkle again lightly with garlic powder, black pepper, and Italian seasoning.

Repeat entire process again with as many layers as you like! Sometimes I only have one layer of veggie burgers and the rest just lasagna, sauce, seasoning and cheese. If it's for my Man, I include another layer of veggie patties. Capishe?

Throw in oven for about 30 to 45 minutes and……………………….

ENJOY!

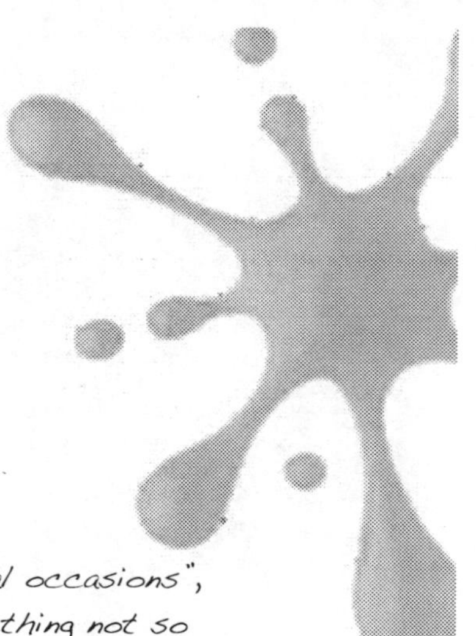

WHAT TO
WEAR TO A SPECIAL OCCASION
IN MY OPINION

Wear any pattern that suits your fancy most of the time - But for " special occasions ", trust me........you will never have remorse if you wear solid colors and something not so revealing or trendy. If you don't follow this simple advise then someday looking back at photos you will say to yourself; " what was I thinking?" LOL LOL LOL Write it down and remember Granny Nancy tried to share it. Capishe?

ANOTHER LITTLE RECIPE TO NOT HAVE REGRET BY ALWAYS TAKING CARE OF YOURSELF, BASICALLY. LOL

Tore up feet are not attractive - what do I mean? You know what I mean, cracked dry heels, heels with blisters, chipped polish, unmanicured toenails etc. etc.
Do you really think nobody notices?
People watchers do.
Men do.
Big deal breaker ladies!
Just a personal opinion of mine - I'm JUST sharing to help you. (people DO look at those things)

It has been said, if a person doesn't take care of their feet, most likely the other areas of their body are being unattended to as well.
EWWWWW, yuk

RECIPE TO IDENTIFY WHEN SOMEONE IS POSSIBLY BEING DISHONEST...

*Are they answering questions you didn't even ask?

*Are they trying really hard to convince you of who they are, what they OR what they have done? Etc etc.......

*Lack of eye contact (everyone knows this one, lol) Or if they are aware that lack of eye contact is a sign of deceit then they will go the opposite direction and make extended eye contact continuously.

*Excessive detail in their stories (answering questions you didn't ask)
Voice changes (this one is tough to pick up on, it will be a vocal pitch while they are talking)

*Hesitation, they will pretend not to hear what you said. Liar's do this a lot.

*Defensive, they become irritable, annoyed because of discomfort.

Opinion Recipe On Judging

Just some little hints, of course there are exceptions to the rule. This is about Judging People, Democrats and Telling your Business.

First On Judging people:
Don't judge others because they are committing different sins than you.
Helloooooooooo.......?

Second On About Democrats:
"Democrats work to help people who need help. That other party, they work for people who don't need help.
That's all there is to it"
~Harry S. Truman

Third On the Best way to not let people know your business is to............
Not post it on the facebook
And Don't tell anyone!

FourthStop telling everybody all about your problems,
Tell God, he has it all figured out.

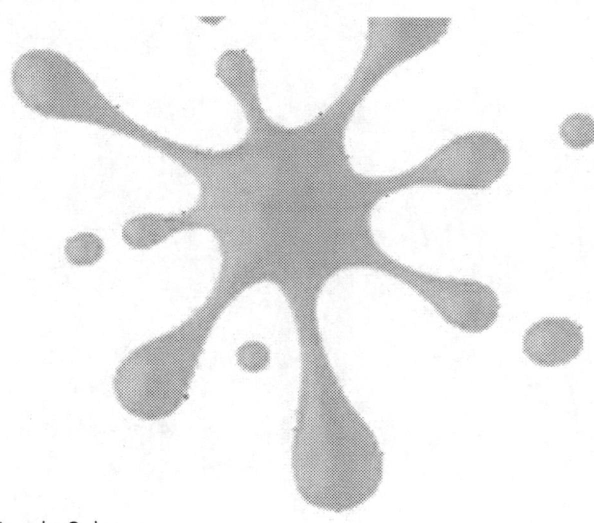

Granny Nancy's Sharp Slammin Simple Salmon

Special Tip:
The fish is done if it flakes easily when tested with a fork.
(insert fork into fish and twist gently)

Ingredients:

4 5 to 6 oz skinless salmon fillets, about 1 inch thick
1 tablespoon olive oil
4 large Roma tomatoes, chopped small
1 tablespoon butter
¼ finely chopped up cilantro
Salt
Lemon Pepper

Directions:

Lightly season Salmon with lemon salt and pepper. Heat olive oil in large non stick skillet over medium-high heat. Add salmon; cook 8 to 10 minutes or until salmon flakes easily when tested with a fork, turn over once halfway through cooking. (if salmon browns to quickly reduce heat to medium).

Transfer salmon to serving platter. Add tomatoes, and butter to skillet; cook and stir 1 minute.

Spoon tomatoes over salmon and sprinkle cilantro on top.

ENJOY!

RECIPE TO BE SUPPORTIVE TO YOUR CHILDREN

Applies to younger children and older children

I will try to make this a simple short recipe for everyone to understand and yet still allow you to be successful at it. Here it goes.........

#1 Omit self serving selfishness.

#2 Support their passion, not what you want their passion to be.

Isn't being supportive easy?
Yay! You can do it!

For the adult child that wants to kick it and refuses to think about tomorrow........

Do not participate in crippling them.......
Also.......Do not budget your butt off, so they don't have to. They don't learn like that.
That makes no sense? They will never ever learn...
And then what about when you are gone?
They will be lost without you, they won't know what to do... (sad face)
We must be strong and think of what is best for them.
Just saying "no" helps your Adult Child.
Don't think of the pleasure you will get by being their hero. (Don't you want them to do better?)
Don't you trust God to answer your prayers?
He is stronger than us and just because you don't know God's plan is no reason to give up on God.
Parents, we taught them everything we know already from the moment they were born.
Now.........
Just hold on, God knows what he is doing.

RECIPE FOR PARENTS OF GROWN CHILDREN TO NOT FALL INTO "GUILT" TRAP

Parental guilt is very lucrative to the child (especially grown children) in many ways. Think about it. Don't let your grown children make you think it's something you did or didn't do that is the cause for their problems and decisions they are making now as adults or decisions they have made in the past. If it is everyday stuff that everybody else has to deal with. Advise them to get over it and move forward like everyone else. It is better. Quit giving them $20 to "help" them delay moving forward.

Navy Beans

Ingredients:

1 Bag of dried northern beans
1 package smoked ham hocks (or smoked turkey legs?)
1 fat onion
Salt and Pepper to taste.
Apple cider vinegar (optional)

Soak Beans in large bowl overnight or at least for a couple of hours – check back of bag. (cover while soaking)

After soaking, pick out any beans that look odd.

Put in large pot, add water so that beans are more than covered, add ham hocks, cover and bring to a boil.

Cover and simmer until done.

To test beans for doneness:

Get a couple of beans on a spoon and blow on them, if the skin cracks- then they are done or if you taste them they should be a bit soft.

Optional: add 1 little capful of vinegar to your individual bowl for a flare of flavor.

Serve with cornbread.

ENJOY!!!

RECIPE TO KEEP YOUR HOME ORDERLY ONCE YOUR CHILDREN BECOME TEENAGERS or are GROWN

(in case you end up with "grown" stay at home kids,? LOL) OR IN CASE THEY MOVE BACK IN FOR AWHILE ?
Stay consistent with the following and maybe they won't want to be a "stay at home child" after all. LOL

The following are some suggestions as to what you can say to implement this recipe:

First and foremost, you must let everyone in the household know you have a statement to make:
A suggestion; initially you could read this clearly to all family members and then follow up by posting on the refrigerator old school style.

#1 WE WILL ALL HONOR THE "10" COMMANDMENTS IN THIS HOUSE AT ALL TIMES.

#2 WE WILL ALL EXERCISE COMMON COURTESY AT ALL TIMES

I don't care if you don't like me or admire me right now, because who you are and who you become as a person is much more important, therefore: while you live here you will practice common courtesy. When I say "good morning" you will say "good morning", as well as to one another. When I say anything you will respond and I will do the same for you. We will all do the same for one another.
While you live here, you will show up for the normal family events just as I will, meals, church, holidays, funerals, weddings and siblings events. You will celebrate our families Birthdays just as we do yours. This includes Grandparents that love you. Call them and if it applies send a card. You will bathe and clean up after yourselves just as I do. We will let each other know about our comings and goings as it is out of courtesy and concern. Curfews will be respected with only a 5 minute grace. We WILL use our phones to notify each other of changes. The only people allowed to live here are people in a relationship with one another. People in relationships talk and respect one another. That's it!

#3 EDUCATION

We wake up. Shower. Brush Teeth. Get dressed! Brush hair. Go to Class!/Go to work. (what ever the case) Turn in your assignments. My expectation of your GPA will vary depending on my assessment of your academic efforts and abilities. But there is no excuse

for not doing the work. Education is on my list of "Willing to Die For" because it is such an accurate indicator of adolescent social and mental health. It is my job to prepare you for life - and I will be doing my job no matter what it takes. When teens are in trouble, grades go plummeting and I am aware of that.
IF YOU ARE NOT GOING TO SCHOOL IN ORDER TO LIVE HERE YOU MUST HAVE A JOB AND CONTRIBUTE. See #7

#4 DRUGS

IF I SUSPECT ANYTHING OF THE SORT, I WILL DO WHAT EVER IT TAKES TO SAVE YOU FROM ADDICTION! IF NEED BE; I WILL QUIT MY JOB. I WILL SEARCH YOUR ROOM. I WILL SPY, SNOOP, RUMMAGE THROUGH YOUR PANTS POCKETS, READ YOUR DIARY, HAVE YOU FOLLOWED OR FOLLOW YOU MYSELF - WHAT EVER IT TAKES! IF NEED BE I WILL BUG YOU AND YOUR ROOM WITH WHATEVER DEVICES ARE AVAILABLE. NOT HAPPENING, GET IT?

#5 VIOLENCE

I welcome your anger, and I promise.....you will sometimes hear mine. But violence is just not what we do in this family. Not with your hands or your words. EVER! I will not degrade you with profanity and you will not degrade me or any of our family members.

#6 SEX

None of my children will have sex in this house or anywhere else as long as they are living at home. That goes for boys and girls! There will be no sex. Never have sex until you are married or until you are grown and no longer living here. Any questions? I can explain all the complications that come along with it, if needed. NO SEX! THAT'S IT!

#7 JOBS

You will work as soon as you are able and you must contribute. It is a way of life, if you want something, you must earn it honestly. Of course you will have to keep our grades up to enjoy the luxury of an income.

Making Homemade Noodles

2 Servings

Prep time: 30 minutes

YOU WILL NEED A "ROLLING PIN" FOR THIS ONE

Ingredients

2/3 to 3/4 cup all-purpose flour

1/8 teaspoon salt

1 egg

1 teaspoon cold water

6 cups water

1 teaspoon canola oil

Directions

In a small bowl, combine 2/3 cup flour and salt. Make a well in the center. Beat egg and cold water; pour into well. Stir together, forming a ball.

Turn dough onto a floured surface; knead for 8 minutes, adding remaining flour if necessary to keep dough from sticking to surface or hands. Cover and let rest for 10 minutes.

On a lightly floured surface, roll dough into a 12-in. x 8-in. rectangle. Dust top of dough with flour to prevent sticking while rolling. Trim the edges. Dust both sides of dough with flour. Roll up jelly-roll style; cut into 1/4-in. slices. Separate and unroll the noodles; let rest on a clean towel for 1 hour.

In a large saucepan, bring water to a rapid boil. Add oil and noodles; cook for 7-9 minutes or until tender. Drain and serve immediately. Yield: 2 servings.

ENJOY!

White Spaghetti and Peas

3 tbsp butter
3 tbsp flour
2 cups milk, heated
4 slices cooked back bacon, cut into thin strips
½ cup green pepper cut into strips
1 tbsp chopped lemon rind
4 portions cooked spaghetti, hot
1 cup grated mozzarella cheese
pinch nutmeg
pinch salt and pepper

Cook Spaghetti, drain and set to the side.

Melt 2 tbsp butter in saucepan over medium heat.
Add flour and mix well with large spoon; cook 3 minutes over low heat, stirring constantly.
Pour in hot milk and mix well; continue cooking 8 to 10 minutes over low heat. Stir frequently.
Sprinkle in nutmeg, season and set white sauce aside.
Melt remaining butter in skillet. Add bacon, green pepper and lemon rind; season well. Cook 3 minutes over medium heat.
Stir in peas, pasta and white sauce. Add cheese, mix well and cook 2 minutes over medium heat before serving.

ENJOY!

Variations of White Sauce

WHITE SAUCE

(With no butter! Yay!)

Ingredients:
1 cup Milk
4 Tablespoons Olive Oil
2 Tablespoons Flour

In a small saucepan over medium heat, heat milk until warm. Do not boil.

In a separate bowl, mix the flour and oil together, then add a small spoonful of the warmed milk at a time, whisking until the mixture is runny and smooth.

Over medium heat, heat the entire mixture, whisking constantly. Turn off the heat at desired consistency. You can add anything to it such as; Cheese, salt & pepper, parsley, garlic or anything you choose.

*****SEE NEXT PAGE FOR VARIATIONS OF THIS WHITE SAUCE*****

VARIATIONS OF WHITE SAUCE
(WHICH CAN BE FOR FISH, MEAT or VEGETABLES)

Sauces add variety to the diet, make foods more attractive to the eye and to the palate, and thus stimulate appetite.

TO MAKE A ROUX;

For a White Sauce – The American method of making a roux for white sauce is to melt the fat, add the flour and cook only until the mixture bubbles before adding the liquid. This saves time, but at the expense of the flavor of the sauce. The French method is to melt the fat, add the flour and cook, with constant stirring, for five minutes, before adding any liquid. This removes the raw taste of the flour.

USE 1 CUP MEDIUM WHITE SAUCE AS THE BASIS FOR EACH SAUCE:

CAPER SAUCE – Add 2 to 4 tablespoons chopped capers.

CELERY SAUCE – Add ½ cup chopped cooked celery.

CHEESE SAUCE – Add 2 to 4 ounces grated cheese. Set over hot water and stir until the cheese is blended with sauce. Season to taste with mustard and paprika.

CREAM GRAVY – Use 2 tablespoons meat drippings for butter in white sauce recipe.

CREAM SAUCE – Use cream instead of milk in white sauce.

EGG SAUCE, NO. 1 – Add 1 hard-cooked egg, chopped.

EGG SAUCE, NO. 2 – Beat uncooked egg, dilute with 1 tablespoon of hot thin white sauce, then beat this into the remainder of a cup of sauce. If the egg white is beaten separately, the sauce will be foamy.

LOBSTER SAUCE – Add ½ cup finely flaked cooked lobster.

MOCK HOLLANDAISE SAUCE – Pour sauce over 2 slightly beaten egg yolks, 2 tablespoons each of butter and lemon juice, beat thoroughly and serve immediately.

MUSHROOM SAUCE – Add ½ to 1/3 cup chopped or sliced cooked mushrooms to sauce.

OLIVE SAUCE – Add ¼ cup chopped or stuffed olives.

OYSTER SAUCE – Heat 1 pint small oysters in their own liquor to boiling point. Remove from heat after they have cooked ½ minute and combine with sauce. Season to taste.

PARSLEY SAUCE – Add 2 to 4 tablespoons chopped parsley.

PIMIENTO SAUCE – Add 2 tablespoons minced onion and 6 tablespoons minced pimiento. Onion may be browned in fat when making white sauce, if desired.

SHRIMP SAUCE – Add ½ cup chopped cooked Shrimp.

SOUBISE SAUCE – Rub 4 boiled onions and 2 sprigs parsley through a course sieve. Combine with sauce.

TOMATO CREAM SAUCE – Cook 1 cup fresh or canned tomatoes, 1 stalk Celery, 1 slice onion, ½ teaspoon salt and a few grains cayenne together for 20 minutes. Rub through a sieve. Add gradually, stirring constantly , to white sauce.

VELOUTE SAUCE – Use 1 cup well seasoned white stock for milk in thin or medium white sauce.

YELLOW SAUCE – Add hot sauce to 1 or 2 slightly beaten egg yolks and beat thoroughly.

RECIPE OF THINGS TO KEEP IN MIND WHEN SHOPPING FOR VARIOUS GROCERIES

Be sure to scrutinize the high end health food and enviro-conscious goods in your grocery cart. Example: Stick with the conventional, NON- organic (aka "cheaper") varieties of bananas, avocados, asparagus and cauliflower, which apparently have fewer pesticides than other fresh products. NOW.....for apples, nectarines, peaches, pears tomatoes, spinach, strawberries, baby food, meat, and chicken, the organic versions are usually worth the higher price tags.

Different ways to save on groceries:

Get out your cutting board and use it ~

You can cut your total down quite a bit if you AVOID pre-chopped, pre-sorted, single serving conveniently packaged foods - such as: bagged Vegetables, pre-sliced cheese?

Or who buys instant oatmeal just because it comes in pre-measured envelopes? Hellloooo. Everybody has a measuring cup. Seriously?

Stop with the "status brands" or just plain "popular brand" already, choose no name brands. Brand X typically is coming from the same place as the status brand, often it's just the packaging that's different. (check the ingredients to confirm) For instance, while shopping, look for your products either on the higher shelves or the lower shelves. Trust me, companies pay for "prime" eye-level placement for a reason. Generics will be up high or down low. Wow! Another savings!

Keep that sponge clean! In this day and age we must think about potentially hazardous bacteria!
Microwave it on high for about 1 minute and then in the dishwasher.

Oh, and the dishrag? Disgusting, it never gets all the way clean. Let it go. It's so Gross.

RECIPE TO NOT ALLOW THE BAD GUY TO MAKE YOU FEEL BAD
THIS IS FOR MAN OR WOMEN

Why do we feel bad for the person who has made US feel bad? You know what I'm saying???............Someone who has repeatedly hurt you? STOP! It's dumb! Don't take it on. (the only thing you can do that makes sense is Pray for them to not continue to do it to others) RECIPE: RUN FROM THAT PERSON.

Urban Chicken Tomato Tacos

Healthy

Make it easy on yourself and pick up an already cooked chicken from any grocery store -or- make it really inexpensive and get one from Sam's or Costco.

(also you may want to buy 2 cans of Tomato sauce and 8 tomatoes so you can have extra left overs for tomorrow night – see next page for the left over recipe called "Pizzaza by Granny")

Ingredients

1 Package Corn Tortilla's
2 cups shredded Chicken
1 can Tomato Sauce
4 Roma Tomatoes
Avocado (optional)
½ white Onion
Cilantro
Baby Spinach (Buy it already washed)
1 Lime
Shredded Cheddar Cheese (or Jack cheese –or cheese of your choice)
Hot Sauce? You decide.

Shred your Chicken, set aside. (depending on how many people. If only about 2 or 3 people a couple of cups will work. (oh! If your'e chicken seems dry? Drizzle some Olive Oil over it – it will make it juicy.

Wash top of Tomato sauce can then open and pour into microwavable bowl, cover so it doesn't splatter inside microwave. Heat for about 2 minutes, stir, cover and set aside.

Wash and dice up Roma Tomatoes and add to the Tomato Sauce and set aside again. (you can add a dash of hot sauce to that too if you like)

Wash Avocado, slice up, lay on small plate.

Peel and cut white onion up in small pieces and put in small bowl.

Rinse Cilantro and cut up stems and all into fine pieces.

CONTINUED ON NEXT PAGE.....................

Cut up Spinach (just like it is lettuce)

Slice open Lime and squeeze over your chicken or your cilantro – take your pick.

Heat your Tortilla for about 30 seconds.

Ok...........so now you have all of your'e ingredients ready!

Get some dinner plates out and put your warm tortilla on a plate,,,,,

Layer your chicken and everything else on your tortilla and...............................

ENJOY!!!!!!

OH AND BTW (by the way)......
Check out the next page for what to do the next night with your left overs that you may still have.
(Chicken Pizzaza)

CHICKEN PIZZAZA BY GRANNY

(you can make this by using left over's from last nights
URBAN CHICKEN TACO TOMATO)
Oh, but you must also buy some Focaccia bread and a couple of other things too–

Pre-heat oven to 400 degrees

Ingredients:

Focaccia Bread
Shredded Chicken
1 can Tomato Sauce
Italian Seasoning
Basil Seasoning –or- Fresh Basil (your choice)
Mozzarella Cheese – Shredded
White Onion – diced
So……………..

Get a pan of some sort. (if you want to keep cleanup to a minimum. Line it with foil.

Pile everything up on the Focaccia Bread.

Sprinkle with the Mozzarella Cheese.

Slide in the oven on top shelf.

Bake for about 10 minutes. (everyone's oven is different – so check after 5 minutes. Keep checking every 2 minutes or so.

When baked to your liking………..serve.

ENJOY!

Just want to repeat this one more time: GREAT FACT FOR HATERS TO KNOW

Blowing out the other persons candle
Won't make your's shine any brighter.

DO YOU WANT TO TRY TO MAKE GROUND TURKEY TASTE OR AT LEAST LOOK SORT OF LIKE GROUND BEEF?

You can Marinate your ground Turkey the day before by mixing in the fennel seed and letting it stay refrigerated for 24 hours. It will make it much more tasty!

Check it out...

Ingredients:

2.5 pounds lean ground Turkey
Garlic Powder
Salt
1 Tablespoon Whole Fennel Seed (you can find this in the spice section)
2 Tablespoons Kitchen Bouquet Seasoning & Gravy Mixture (you will usually find this in the spice section as well)
2 Tablespoons Soy Sauce

Get medium to large frying pan.

To the pan add your ground Turkey.

Set your burner to about Medium.

Use large cooking spoon to kind of chop the ground turkey as it cooks.

To the ground Turkey, add Fennel Seeds.

Sprinkle Garlic Powder over Ground Turkey. Don't be too shy with the Garlic powder.
Salt and Pepper the Ground Turkey as it cooks.

Do not add anything else till you see all the ground turkey is all the way cooked. Ok? Capishe?
Once the ground turkey is completely cooked, (you will notice because it kind of turns a brownish color, Remember it is important to make sure it is all the way cooked because it is poultry. Ok? I mean it's not like there is such a thing as "rare" poultry. (Just a little lesson for those who don't know about cooking)
Anyway back to once the ground turkey is completely cooked you can add:
Kitchen Bouquet Seasoning & Soy sauce.
Be sure to stir everything together very well.
NOW, DOESN'T THAT LOOK KIND OF LIKE GROUND BEEF?
There you have it, you can use this for Tacos, Sloppy Joe's, Spaghetti Sauce and a million other things. You decide.

Enjoy!!!!

Big Fat Italian Soul Food Dinner
with French Bread & Kool Aid

#1 For starters, pre-heat oven to 450
#2 Make your Kool Aid so it can begin to chill. (flavor is your option)

#3 Make your easy 1-2-3 Garlic bread (either buy already made) OR............. BUY some French bread already sliced, spread butter on each slice (NOT margarine) then sprinkle with Garlic powder. Then when the time is right, (shortly before the rest of your meal is cooked) broil for about 1 minute. That's 1-2-3- fast garlic bread! LOL

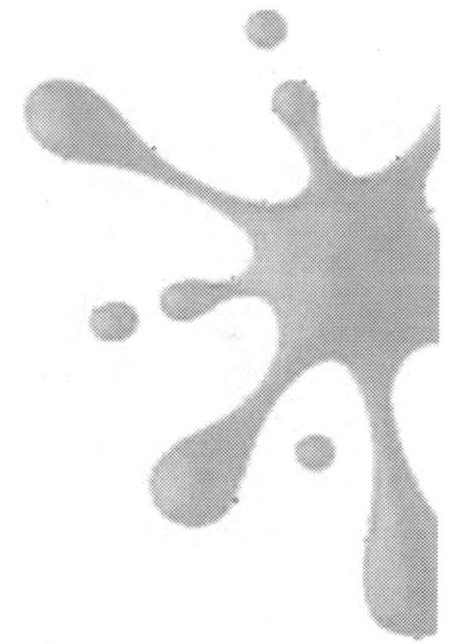

4 Chicken Boneless Chicken Breast
1 package Hot Links
2 Cups uncooked Rice
6 Campari Fresh Tomatoes on the Vine (or Roma Tomatoes)
1 White Onion
1 can 14.5 ounces Diced Tomatoes
Olive Oil
Vegetable Oil
Butter
Garlic Powder
Tony Chachere's Original Creole Seasoning
Mediterranean Basil (Trader Joe)
Salt
Pepper
Water
Kool-Aid – Flavor is your choice – LOL
French Bread

Wash Chicken Breast and season with Garlic Powder, Salt, and Pepper on both sides. Then, bake in oven for 20 minutes @ 450 and remove @ 20 minutes exactly. (of course cut through center of the thickest one and make sure there is no pink juices.

Cut up Hot Links and set aside.

Make Rice according to directions on Rice package, and keep warm on the side. You choose how much you need to make, maybe about 2 cups?

Wash and cut up Tomatoes in quarters – set aside.
Wash top of the can of Tomatoes before opening, then open can and set aside with the fresh tomatoes.

Chop White Onion – not too small, not to big, set aside.
Get big fat frying pan and pour in about 1/4 cup of Olive Oil.
To the Olive Oil, add about 1/8 cup of Vegetable Oil.

To the Olive Oil – Add about 4 slices of Butter.
To the Olive Oil and vegetable oil and Butter add some Garlic Powder, salt and pepper.
Turn burner on medium and sauté a bit.
To all of the above add the Hot Links and sauté.
Now.......to all of that.............
Add the Tomatoes
Add the white Onions
Add the Tony Cachere's Seasoning and the Basil.
Add the Chicken (you may want to cut the Chicken breast in half (or quarters – your option)
Place lid on top and sauté on Medium for about 10-15 minutes.

Serve over Rice.

ENJOY!

Pasta Dish (meatless)
With homemade breadcrumbs on top. YUM!
Extra Extra EZ

This is for any type of crowd. This dish will be from your heart and everyone will love it!

Ingredients:

Loaf of French Sourdough Bread (or something similar)
Extra Virgin light Olive Oil
Salt
Garlic Powder
Flat Pasta Noodles
Cherry Tomatoes (a lot)
Basil (preferably fresh basil – but if you can't find it, then of course you can substitute with dried Basil)

Pre-heat oven to 375

Cut up the Basil real small and set aside.
Wash Tomatoes and let drain.
Cut each little Tomato in half just once.
Set Tomatoes aside.
Get out big Colander and set aside. (to drain pasta noodles)
In large pot, boil some water with a dash or two of Salt.
Follow directions on Pasta package. IMPORTANT: Do not overcook. It is important to only cook for specified time and then remove from boiling water immediately.

Once pasta is cooked for the exact amount of minutes that the package suggest then pour all out into colander.
Once drained, (do not rinse) pour pasta back into the pot and add all the Cherry Tomatoes.
To the pasta add the cut up Basil and some Olive Oil.

Now, toss the pasta, tomatoes and basil all together and sprinkle some salt. Go easy on the salt.

Pour into your big bowl and sprinkle the Bread Crumbs on the top. Or........everybody can just add to their individual bowls of pasta! Yay! LOL

Read below to prepare the Bread Crumbs...

Break up Bread into broken up pieces.
Toss in Big mixing bowl or..... if you need to use a big pot. Do what you have to do.
Drizzle with Olive Oil and toss around like a salad to ensure you get olive oil on every little crumb. Don't drench them, ok?
Spread across a cookie sheet or something similar. (just spread out, that's the main thing)
Once they are all laid out, sprinkle them with the Garlic Powder.
Now, sprinkle lightly with a bit of Salt. Don't over do the salt!
Bake at 350 degrees for about 8 to 10 minutes.
After about 4 minutes of baking, get a spatula and scoop around a bit (kind of turn them over)
Then let finish baking for a couple more moments.

Once you have put this in a beautiful bowl, it is ready to be served.

ENJOY!

Pasta Garlic

Serves 2

If necessary increase the ingredients.............

Kosher Salt
1/4 cup extra virgin Olive Oil
1/2 pound of Spaghetti
3 Garlic Cloves, thinly sliced
A pinch of crushed red pepper flakes
2 Tablespoons chopped fresh parsley or more to taste

Bring a large pot of well salted water to a boil. Add the spaghetti and cook until it is al dente, about 9 minutes. Drain, reserving 1 cup of Pasta water.

While spaghetti is cooking, heat the olive oil in a sauté pan over medium heat. Add the garlic and sauté for 1 minute or until it sizzles. Add the red pepper flakes. Continue sautéing until the edges of the garlic just begin to brown, about 2 more minutes. Add reserved cup of pasta water and a pinch of salt. Continue cooking for 5 minutes, stirring occasionally.

Turn the heat down to medium-low, then add the drained pasta and parsley. Toss until the pasta has absorbed most of the liquid, about 3 minutes.

Serve immediately and.................................

ENJOY!

CHICKEN FINGERS
PARMESAN – CRUSTED

HEALTHY

Believe it or not – this will taste just like
that Greasy-Fast-Food Classic that we love!

Preheat oven to 425 degrees

Things you'll need:

Olive Oil or Vegetable Cooking Spray
2/3 cup Panko (Japanese-style) Bread-Crumbs (find in asian section @ the store).
¼ grated Parmesan Cheese
2 Tablespoons chopped fresh Parsley (optional)
¼ teaspoon ground black pepper
1 tablespoon Dijon mustard
2 eggs whites
1 pound Chicken Tenders

Put your rack in the top third of your oven.
Set a wire rack of some sort on top of a baking sheet and coat the rack lightly with cooking spray.
In a shallow bowl, stir together the breadcrumbs, Parmesan Cheese, Parsley (optional) and Pepper.
In another shallow bowl, whisk together the mustard and egg whites until frothy and kind of like an opaque color.
Now, dip each chicken tender in the egg white mixture, then in the breadcrumb mixture to coat all sides.
Then place on the prepared sprayed rack.
With the cooking spray, spritz the top of each chicken tender "lightly" and evenly, then turn and repeat on the other side of the chicken tender.
Bake until the crumb coating is golden brown and crisp and the chicken is no longer pink in the center.
(you can cut one chicken tender in the middle to check for pink after 15 minutes, this is important)

You will bake about 15 to 20 minutes.

Serve immediately. (this makes about 4 servings)

ENJOY!

BIG PHAT CRAZY FACT

THE FACT THAT YOU'RE STRESSED HAS YOU STRESSED! LOL

RECIPE TO PREVENT YOUR SON FROM EVER TRYING TO WEAR SAGGY PANTS

GET THIS (for all that don't know) HELLOOoooo
"The saggy pants bit started in prison - saggy pants are a display of "availability" for "Anal sex". TELL EVERY BOY, DUDE, MAN THAT YOU KNOW - So they can get it and so they don't all give us that thought, why do they want us to think that they want Anal sex? Ewwww!

Tuna Steaks
(you can cook these on your George Foreman too)

Things you'll need:

Tuna Steaks
Olive Oil
Butter
Lemon
Lime (you will use zest grated on top for garnish)
Salt
Pepper
Cinnamon
Chili Powder

Citrus Sauce for Tuna Steaks

1 tablespoon Butter in Sauté Pan
1 tablespoon Olive Oil
Juice of 1 Lemon
Pinch of Salt
Pinch of Pepper
Pinch of Cinnamon
Pinch of Chili Powder

Sauté really good stirring for a couple of minutes on low and cover with top.
Meanwhile:
Rub Tuna Steak with Olive Oil and Season with Pepper and Garlic Powder.
Sear on George Foreman Grill. MAKE SURE THIS IS ON A DRY GRILL, NO OLIVE OIL OR NOTHING. Just DRY, ok?
When done, you are ready to SERVE!
Drizzle Sauce over Tuna Steak and Grate Lime on Top!
This recipe came from a Girl..............what can I say?

ENJOY!

RECIPE TO BE HAPPY

Don't change so people will like you, be yourself and the "right" people will just love you!

On Being a Lady

Be sure to cut on the bathroom tap water to conceal any less-than-ladylike sounds.

A lady uses privacy to do her makeup, tend to personal hygiene and the sort of things your man (or man to be) doesn't need to know about, thus keeping the mystery to a certain degree.

RECIPE TO NOT SAY THINGS YOU DON'T MEAN

Be very careful of what you say........

Aunt Carol once told me a story that someone told her....... about how you cannot put toothpaste back into the tube, right?

The same applies to words, we can't put them back in our mouth.

Once they have been said and heard , they can be forgiven but not

Forgotten.

(The truth is you have to think the thought before the words roll off your tongue, so stop yourself. We all have the power to stop ourselves.

God gave it too us. Let's be grateful of that.

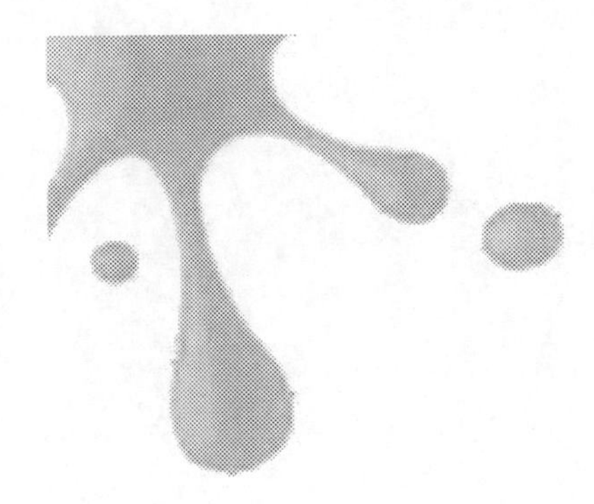

QUICKY CHICKEN SLIDERS

1 Rotisserie Chicken, Shredded (just pick up an already cooked one at the store to make it easy if you like)

2 cups shredded Coleslaw mix

Bar-B-Q Sauce (you choose your favorite)

Black Pepper

Package of Dinner Rolls, Split. (Sweet Hawaiian ones are so tasty!)

Mix your shredded Chicken with the Bar-B-Q sauce and mix together in a sauce pan and heat up.

Place the Barb-B-Q mixed Chicken onto the bottom half of the dinner Rolls and then top with the Coleslaw mix.

Place the other half of dinner roll on the top!

ENJOY!

RECIPE ON HOW TO NOT GIVE ANOTHER PERSON THE RECIPE ON HOW TO ABUSE YOU. THIS IS DEEP! READ OVER AND OVER AND SHARE WITH EVERYONE YOU KNOW.

"Discourse on Voluntary Servitude"

He who domineers over you has only two eyes, only two hands, only one body, no more than is possessed by the least man.

He has indeed nothing more than the power that you confer upon him to destroy you.

Where has he acquired enough eyes to spy upon you if you do not provide them yourselves?

How can he have so many arms to beat you with, if he doesn't borrow them from you?

The feet that trample down your cities, where does he get them if they are not your own?

How does he have any power over you except through you?

by: Etienne De La Boetie
Year: 1558

RECIPE FOR HOW TO FALL IN LOVE

YOU WILL NEVER KNOW LOVE, IF YOU DON'T SURRENDER TO IT.

My Dad once said, "everyone has the "Love Life" they want". So basically you decide. Open your heart.

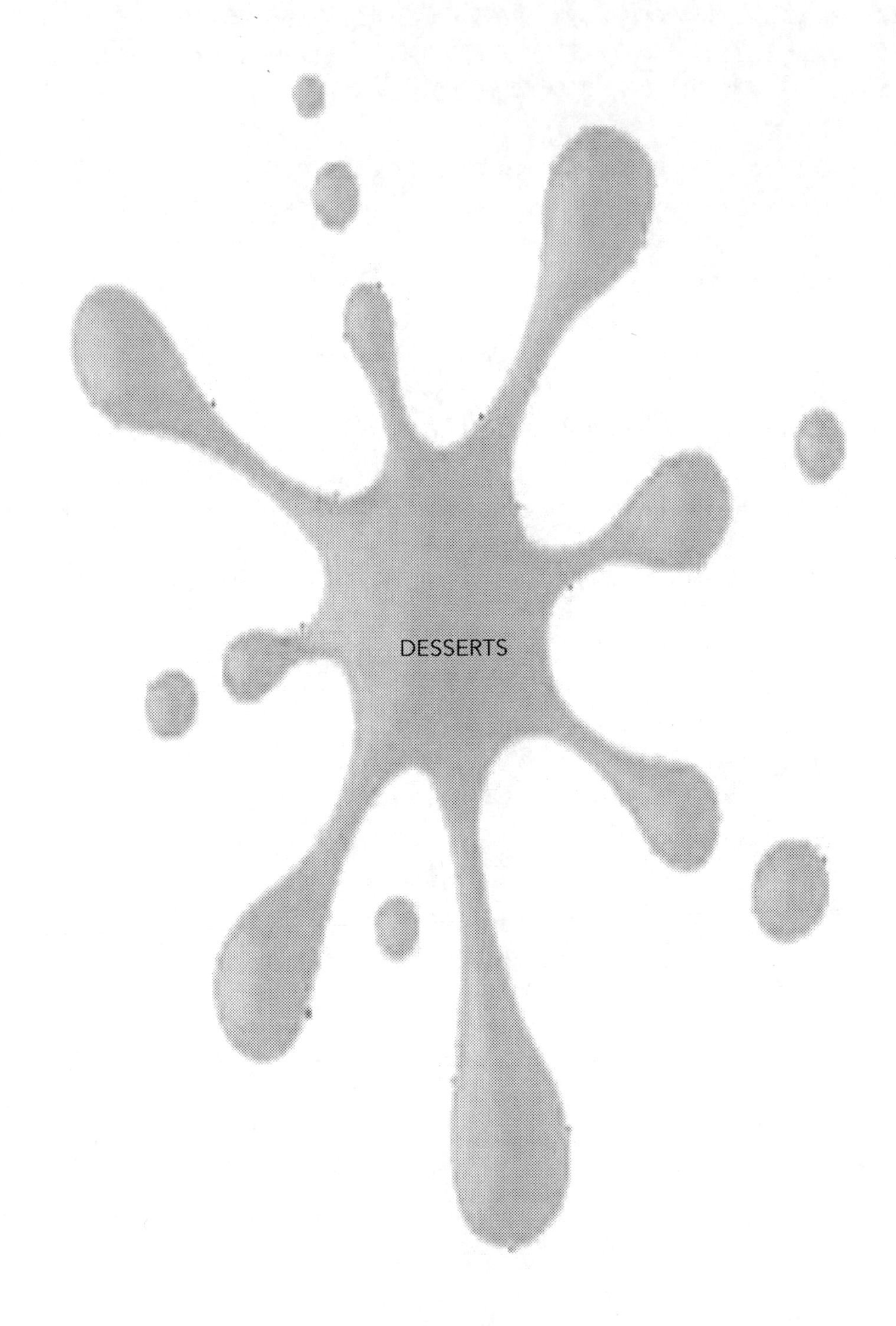

DESSERTS

PEANUT BUTTER FUDGE

Things you'll need:

1 stick of butter
2 cups of sugar
1 can (14 ounces) sweetened condensed milk
1 jar (7 ounces) marshmallow crème
1 jar (16 ounces) peanut butter

Grease 9 X 9 inch pan or a baking dish

In a large pot over medium heat, melt butter.

Add the sugar and condensed milk, bring to a boil and cook for 5 minutes, stirring constantly. Remove from heat and add marshmallow crème and peanut butter. Stir mixture until blended.

Pour mixture into prepared pan and cool for 1 hour, or until fudge is set. Cut into squares and serve.

ENJOY!

RECIPE TO HAVE THE RIGHT FRAME OF MIND WHEN LOOKING FOR LOVE

Different friends, people or should I say I hear people often, single people (women especially) saying they can't find a man that meets their criteria often saying they want to find somebody that can afford them? Meaning that somebody has to be financially well off? Financially secure? Are those women financially secure? It really depends on what age group your'e talking about, k'mon. Don't expect more out of who your'e looking for than you expect out of yourself, hellooooo?

What do I tell them?

Money is not going to love you back! Look for someone -NOT- something.

1-2-3 Shortbread Cookies

Pre-heat oven to 275

Things you'll need;

1 pound butter, room temperature
1 cup sugar
5 cups all-purpose flour

In large mixing bowl, cream butter and sugar until light and creamy.

Add flour one cup at a time until blended. Dough will be thick and barely stick together.

Press dough evenly into a 9 X 13 inch pan. Using a fork, prick dough to bottom of pan, in one inch intervals.

Bake for 1 hour. Cut dough into small bars and continue baking for 15 more minutes.

Cool and then store in air tight container.

ENJOY!

Carrot Cake
Glenda Cake

Preheat oven to 350

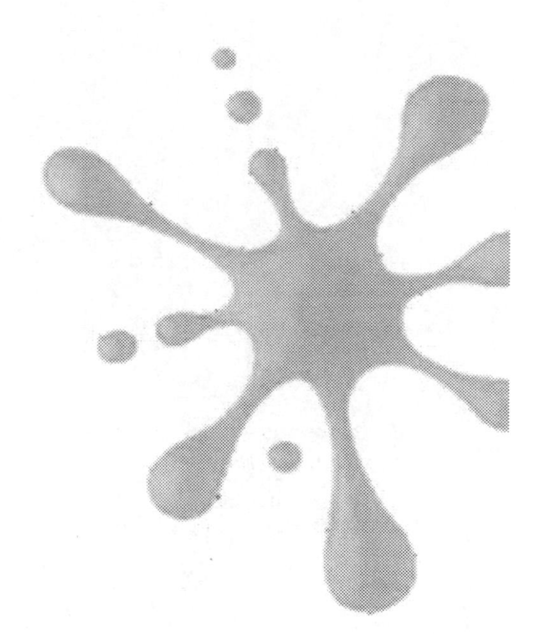

Ingredients:

2 cups Sugar
4 eggs
1 ½ cup vegetable oil
2 cups of flour
2 tsp cinnamon
2 tsp baking soda
1 tsp salt
2 cups carrots
1 8 oz. can crushed pineapple
1 cup chopped walnuts (optional)
Raisins (optional)

Cream together the sugar, eggs and vegetable oil, set aside.
Mix together the flour, cinnamon, baking soda and salt. Set aside.
Mix together carrots, crushed pineapple, chopped walnuts and raisins.
Now……mix together the carrots, pineapple, walnuts and raisins along with the sugar, eggs and vegetable oil.
To that, add the flour cinnamon, salt and baking soda.
Using mixer beat all ingredients together. (no need to beat to long)
Pour into Oblong cake pan and bake at 350 for about 35 minutes. (ovens vary, so check and if need be cook another 3 to 5 minutes and check again.
Remove from oven and let cool a couple of hours before frosting. (actually, refrigerate and then frost)

Cream Cheese Frosting
(you may want to double this recipe if you love frosting)

1 block cream cheese (8 oz.)
1/3 cup powdered sugar
2 tsp vanilla

Cream all ingredients together and once cake is cool frost cake.

ENJOY!!!!!

7 UP CAKE

Preheat oven to 325 degrees

3 sticks Butter
3 cups of Sugar
Cream together 20 minutes,
Add 5 eggs, one at a time
Add 3 cups Flour
2 tablespoons Lemon Extract
Fold in ¾ cup 7 UP

Pour into well greased 12 cup Bundt Pan.

Bake at 325 degrees for 1 to about 1 ¼ hours.

ENJOY!

RECIPE TO MAKE THINGS BETTER IN YOUR LIFE.

Make the decision to make better decisions.
(It's that simple)
(or at least it's a start)

REALLY GOOD FAST CAKE

Pre Heat Oven to 350 degrees

1 Stick of Butter
1 ½ Teaspoon Vanilla Butter Flavoring
½ cup Sugar
1 cup Sour Cream
¼ cup Vegetable Oil
3 eggs
1 Box Cake mix (preferably Duncan Hines Butter cake mix)

Mix all together and Bake in Bundt pan for approx.
35 to 45 minutes. (after 35 minutes, keep checking if fork comes out of middle clean, then it's a done deal.

ENJOY!

RECIPE TO BE IN LOVE FOREVER AND EVER

Be with someone who you love and adore!
Be with someone who adores you and loves you too!
It doesn't get any better than that!

So don't get with someone who you don't love just to be with somebody!

Brownie Smores

You determine how many.
This is just for 4 Smores.

Pre heat oven to 350 degrees

4 Graham Crackers (whole)
8 little Brownies
Chocolate Sauce
8 large Marshmallows

Place 4 Graham Crackers on cookie sheet.

Place Brownies on top of each Graham Cracker

Place 1 Marshmallow on top of each Brownie.

Place in oven for about 2 ½ minutes or until you see Marshmallow is melted.

Remove from oven and carefully place Graham Cracker on plate.

Drizzle each cracker with Chocolate sauce.

ENJOY!

RECIPE TO NEVER GET A DUI

Of course, don't drink and drive. It's that simple. However, some people need to hear it another way after a couple of drinks.........

Do not even plan to have a drink if you go somewhere and you are driving.
If you do have a drink, you must remember 2 things:

1. Don't drive

2. If you are being ignorant because your'e drunk then if someone tells you you shouldn't drive, you must listen. Basically, once you have had more than 1 drink.................driving becomes risky.

REMEMBER THIS:
You cannot make good decisions while you are intoxicated. Especially driving decisions.! Helloooo.!!! How can you decide it's ok to drive if your thinking is distorted, hazy, fuzzy, imprecise, unclear? If someone else says you shouldn't drive then you need to listen. They have a better view of you than you have of yourself at that moment. Get it? PLEASE REMEMBER THIS.

FLOURLESS CHOCOLATE CAKE

Here's the deal: If you use a food processor the texture of this cake is going to be DELICATE and DECADENT!
This cake can be baked in a small cake pan, or divided among muffin cups.

Heat oven to 350 degrees

Ingredients:
Whipped Cream (to put on top of the cake, I love it like that!)
½ cup sliced Almonds
2 tablespoons Sugar
12 ounces Dark Chocolate Chips (get some good ones)
½ cup (1 stick) unsalted Butter
4 Eggs
6 inch cake pan or muffin tins
Cooking spray that contains flour.

Spritz a 6-inch cake pan or your muffin tins with baking spray containing Flour.

In a food processor, pulse the almonds and sugar until finely ground. Set aside.

In a glass bowl, or measuring cup, combine the chocolate chips and butter. Microwave on high in 15-second bursts, stirring between, until melted and smooth.

With the processor running, pour the chocolate mixture in and process until combined. One at a time, add the eggs, processing between each to combine. Scrape down the sides of the bowl and process one last time. Pour the batter into the prepared pan.
Bake for 15 to 25 minutes. (depending on pan size, so keep close watch!) or until the cake is puffed and no longer glossy. Let rest in the pan until the top sinks back down, about 10 minutes. Invert onto a plate.

Serve warm or at room temperature.
Makes 6 servings.

Start to finish 30 minutes

ENJOY !

CREAMY FRUIT SALAD FOR ROOKIES

Ingredients:

½ cup chopped Strawberries
½ cup Blueberries
½ cup green Grapes
1 small 3 –ounce can Mandarin Oranges, drained
1 tablespoon Honey
1 cup Whipped Topping

Combine Strawberries, Blueberries, Grapes and Oranges in a medium bowl.

Add Honey and mix well.

Add the whipped topping by gently folding the fruit over the topping until well mixed.

Refrigerate and serve chilled.

ENJOY!

RECIPE TO RECOGNIZE WHEN SOMEONE YOU LOVE NEEDS YOUR UNDERSTANDING

When someone's behavior changes, (someone close to you especially) maybe you can't figure out why their behavior has changed? Stop and take into account what is going on in that persons life, or perhaps something is happening that they haven't shared with you? But the bottom line is something is going on that is causing them to have different behavior. Just stop and think about what has been going in the past couple of months or so? Take the time to be perceptive. Give them a break and be that understanding force in their life, be understanding just like God does for ALL of us every single day. Remember not to take it personal and keep in mind it is not about you. Capishe?

RECIPE TO MOVE ON IN LIFE

Remember this:

Your past only becomes your present if you let it.

(That's all it takes! Recognize it and move on. Yay!)

RECIPE FOR HOW TO GET THE LITTLE EGG SHELLS THAT ACCIDENTALLY WENT INTO THE EGG WHEN YOU CRACKED IT OPEN...

~~~First of all, when ever you are going to crack eggs open for any recipe or (even just to scramble or cook eggs)
Be sure to crack open into a clear glass bowl. This will allow you to see clearly any little shells that are in there.
~~~Now, if some shell gets into the eggs, take a piece of the egg shell and scoop it up. The little egg shell will gravitate towards the egg shell which will allow you to scoop it out and get rid of it. If you try to use your fingers or anything else then that little egg shell will run from you for a long time! LOL The little egg shell will not run from the big eggs shell. Helloooooo
This is a true fact.

Lionel Douglass
(The best husband on the planet, just sayin) I love that Man!

JAVE MOCHA ICE-CREAM LOVE

Tanya La Bahn

This is the longest recipe I know, but there is no other like it, so give it a shot!

This next cake is for all you Starbuck Junkies.
I don't know where I got the recipe from.
I just know I have been making this for a long time.
Everyone is going to love it!

Preparation time will be about 40 minutes.
Freeze time will be 9 hours.
This will make about 8 to 10 servings.

¼ CUP hot strong Coffee
1 tablespoon Coffee Liqueur (optional)
1 teaspoon Sugar
18 to 20 Ladyfingers, split in half horizontally
1 8-ounce package cream cheese, softened
¼ cup Sugar
1 teaspoon Vanilla
1 /1/2 cups vanilla Ice Cream
½ cup miniature semisweet chocolate pieces
1 pint Coffee Ice Cream
1 ½ cups Fudge ice-cream topping

Chill two medium mixing bowls.
Line a 5-cup round-bottomed bowl or mold with plastic wrap, letting the edges of the wrap hang over the sides of the bowl or mold.

In a shallow bowl combine the hot coffee and the coffee Liqueur and the 1 teaspoon sugar; stir to dissolve sugar. Brush rounded sides of ladyfingers with the coffee mixture.

Line the bottom and side of the bowl or mold with Ladyfingers, placing the rounded side outward. Fill any gaps with Ladyfinger trimmings so that the lining is solid. Drizzle with any remaining coffee mixture Reserve remaining ladyfingers. Cover and chill the lined bowl or mold until needed.

In a medium mixing bowl beat cream cheese, the ¼ cup of sugar, and the vanilla with an electric mixer on medium speed until fluffy. Now set aside.

In 1 of the chilled bowls stir vanilla ice cream, pressing it against the side of bowl with a spoon just till softened (do not let ice cream get too soft).

Immediately fold the softened vanilla ice cream and chocolate pieces into the cream cheese mixture; cover and freeze for 3 to 4 hours or until stiff, stirring mixture occasionally so chips don't sink.
Spread cream cheese mixture over the ladyfingers in the bowl or mold, spreading up the sides, to make lining. Cover with heavy foil and freeze for 2 to 4 hours till firm.

In the other chilled bowl soften coffee ice cream as directed. Spoon on top of the cream cheese mixture, spreading smoothly. Cover surface of the dessert completely with the remaining ladyfingers.

Fold excess plastic wrap over surface. Cover tightly with heavy foil. Freeze until firm or up to 1 month.

To serve Remove foil and invert dessert onto a serving platter; remove bowl or mold and plastic wrap. Let stand at room temperature for 20 minutes or so to soften lightly before cutting.

Don't forget to get out a small sauce pan and heat the Coffee-Hot-Fudge Sauce ice cream topping.

Drizzle each slice with some of the sauce.

ENJOY! ENJOY! ENJOY! ENJOY!

RECIPE TO REALIZE JUST BECAUSE YOU HAVE BEEN IN THAT RELATIONSHIP FOR A LONG TIME DOESN'T MEAN YOU HAVE TO STAY in it?! LIKE IT'S A PRISON SENTENCE OR SOMETHING?

For some reason, many people actually believe the longer and harder they try to make a bad relationship work that it will deem them as "strong" because they stayed so long? PULL-EEEEZE! You have been fooled! It takes more strength to move on. Don't be a Lunatic! Recognize it for how it really is. Life and time is Precious.

Create yourself some new yesterdays starting today.

This goes for just regular friendship relationships too! Are you the only one who is being a good friend? If the other person isn't......then whats the purpose? You ain't going to get a friendship award. Just sayin.........

Recipe to Understand Reasons to Cut the Apron Strings.

Children have figured out how to make us as parents feel as though we must continuously prove our love to them. Sometimes they continue to need us financially or emotionally or both and that's ok but we have to have boundaries. Because there can come a time when it's all about proving our love and this gets unhealthy for the child requesting the proof. K'mon! You must let them know that one day you will be gone and then what? We don't know our tomorrows, we don't know if we even have tomorrow regardless of our age? The main thing is for your own emotional health, remember this; we want our children to be able to go on and be independent should heaven call us to come home tomorrow. Right? So......make your decisions based on what will be best for your children to always be independent - so.....be strong and let them make the mistakes they need to make and resolve things on their own. As a matter of a fact, you may even want to let them know about TMI. This younger generation sometimes tells us way too much. Know what I'm saying? Do they tell us so we can worry for them???? Think about that.....................

PLUMP POUND CAKE

Preheat oven to 300 Degrees

Ingredients:

3 cups Sugar
3 cups Flour
2 cups Soft Butter (room temperature softened – not melted from heating it, ok? Capishe?)
¼ cup of Milk
11 eggs
1 tablespoon Lemon (or vanilla – your choice)

Cream Sugar and Butter.
Add Eggs (one at a time)
Add flour, alternating with adding milk.
Add Vanilla.

Bake at 300 degrees for 1 hour and 30 minutes in bundt cake pan.

ENJOY!

RECIPE TO NOT FEEL GUILTY FOR YOUR GROWN CHILDREN'S CHOICES

If you were a good parent and you did a good job, the best you could at raising your child then any choices your child makes as a grown person is not because of anything you did or didn't do.

So, no need to feel guilty.

It about reminding them they must take accountability for their choices and we can't do that for them.

They just need to hear us continue to teach them life lessons through conversation.

Recipe to know when NOT to talk on your cell phone

Do not talk on your cell phone in public. That is it. Go step aside somewhere. Nobody wants to hear your conversations. (why do some people get loud as soon as they get on the cell phone?) Do you think you will look important? Everybody know what your'e up to, hellooo! So, if you have to accept a call and you are in public, do so quietly at least., and step aside. Oh, and if you are at the cash register and people are waiting and the cashier is tending to you, get off the phone so you can hurry up with your transaction already. Oh and also, the person on the other end of the phone doesn't want to hear you talk to the cashier, or the worker in the store or whoever............. Geez. Just sayin.............

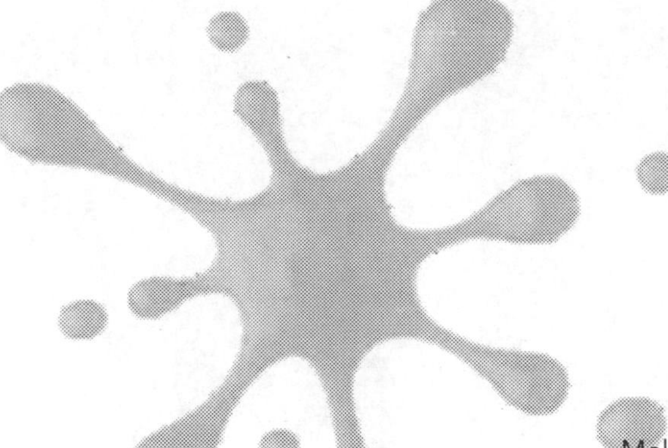

Truffles

Makes about 30 (1 ounce) Truffles

6 ounces unsweetened Chocolate, chopped
1 ½ cups heavy Cream
½ teaspoon Orange Extract
2 Tablespoons plus ½ Teaspoon Saccharin
Unsweetened cocoa powder for dusting
6 ounces chopped Dark Chocolate, at least 60% cocoa
in the bowl of a food processor

Heat cream in a saucepan over medium heat until small bubbles appear around the edge. Pour cream over chocolate and allow to stand for 30 seconds. Blend until mixture is smooth. Add orange extract and Saccharin. Transfer mixture to a shallow dish and refrigerate until hard, at least 1 hour.

Using a 1-ounce portion scoop or a tablespoon, scoop out balls of chocolate and pace on a baking sheet. Place sheet in the refrigerator for about 30 minutes.

When chilled, roll each truffle in the palm of your hand into a perfect round.

Drop truffles into cocoa powder to finish.

Store truffles refrigerated in an airtight container.

For a slightly more indulgent treat, after coating the truffles in cocoa powder, coat them in dark chocolate. Melt 6 ounces chopped dark chocolate (at least 60% cocoa) in a double boiler until smooth. Using a skewer or toothpick, spear each truffle and dip into the melted chocolate. Allow the excess coating to drip off, and use a second toothpick to push the truffle onto a sheet pan lined with wax or parchment paper. Refrigerate until coating has hardened.

ENJOY!

ON DATING

(for women who are seeking a lifelong love, a husband, or a father for their children, well........anything long term should I say)?

A good rule of thumb in my opinion.............

Think twice about men who are philanderers and who make no attempt to hide their infidelity or even the ones who attempt to hide it......these could be considered pretentious playboys.

Think twice about men who really believe clubs are the only manner of socializing/mingling and his only means of interacting with others? I mean, of course sometimes but that's all he knows? This could indicate his priority is mainly pleasure seeking?

Also........moving on to older, let's say 40 and up? If they lie about their age and they have never been married? Hmmmmm?

Just look out, that's all I'm saying.

Also, how about keeping one eye open if they are 50 years old and just got a new little sports car? Perhaps they missed something in their youth? They may not be ready for a serious relationship if they are going through a new phase in their life.

Or you may even want to listen carefully and make a note to pay attention to a man who continuously clings to his glory days, he may be stuck and unable to move past that if he hasn't yet, he may never move on. Who knows?

Oh! And don't go for looks as they can be deceiving.

And don't go for wealth, remember money can't love you back.

Of course like I said if you are just dating for a hobby then, I don't know what to say.
LOL

THERE ARE A LOT OF GOOD MEN!

I feel as though there are a lot more GOOD men than the contrary, so know that and if you meet one, be grateful for them and treat them like kings as those good men deserve the best and so do you. So when you are dating, consider;

Men who know God
Men who flatter you,
Men who are not intimidated by you
Men who like your children
Men who make your heart smile
Men who recognize who you are and appreciate you
Men who are clean
Men who help you
Men who respect you
Men who work
Men who adore you
Men who you adore

The list goes on AND ON..................the main thing is if you meet the right someone, REMEMBER :

We get what we give.

I always say don't expect anything out of anybody that you don't expect out of yourself.

Disclosure: Everything I write goes for women as well as men. Both genders deserve what is right. Just my thoughts.

<u>WORTHY OF NOTE QUOTES</u>

""I would rather live my life as if there is a God and die to find out there isn't, than live my life as if there isn't and die to find out there is."
_ALBER CAMUS

The need to be right is the sign of a vulgar mind. -ALBERT CAMUS

"Those who lack the courage will always find a philosophy to justify it".
-ALBERT CAMUS

REAL LIVE
STRAWBERRY SHORTCAKE
(see the Shortcake itself on next page)

(Lemon juice and sugar bring out the natural juices in the berries)

FOR THE STRAWBERRIES:
4 pints strawberries, lightly rinsed, hulled and halved
1 tablespoons fresh Lemon juice
1 tablespoon Sugar

2 cups heavy Cream
1 tablespoon Sugar
6 Shortcakes (see recipe)
6 whole strawberries, for garnish

Place strawberries in a bowl. Sprinkle with lemon juice and sugar, then gently toss with a rubber spatula. Let rest for 1 ½ to 2 hours for juices to develop.

Just before serving, whip cream with 1 tablespoon SUGAR until it holds soft peaks. Set aside inside frig to keep chilled.

THE SHORTCAKE ITSELF

Pre heat oven to 400

Ingredients:

4 cups of Bisquick
½ cup of Sugar
1 ½ cups of Milk
2 Tablespoons melted Butter
1 ½ Teaspoon Almond flavoring

Mix the Bisquick, Sugar, Milk, Butter, and Almond flavoring in a medium size bowl and pour into 12 well greased muffin tins. Bake for 15 to 20 minutes until done and remove from the oven. Cool for 5 minutes and pop out of pans.

To serve, slice off the top third of each shortcake. Place the bottoms on 6 dessert plates and top with 1/3 cup of the prepared berries and juice, plus a spoonful of whipped cream. Cover with the top. Spoon over more berries and juice, then dollop with whipped cream. Garnish each with a whole berry and drizzle with any remaining juice.
ENJOY!

Recipe for Giving a Public Toast

Ok, so here's the deal:

Many situations in life call for a formal "Celebration". While it's fun being part of the celebratory group, it's not always fun being the responsible one for one part of the party. That would be: "The Official Toast". This requires at least one brave soul to stand before a crowd and offer a few words. While some excel at such social situations, others may shutter at the idea, getting tongue-tied and flustered.

So here is a recipe to help you deliver a perfectly articulated toast.
Write your toast as you read the following..........

First acknowledge everyone in attendance to draw your audience in.

Make them feel included and thank them for coming.

Then offer a sincere thanks to the people responsible for pulling the event together.

Now........think about the person or reason you are celebrating.

Is there a well-known quote or joke that instantly comes to mind?

If so.....both are easy transitions to the next part of the toast.

Honoring the person or reason for the event. This can be short and sweet or as lengthy as you wish, so long as the message is honest and comes from the heart.

A few more important tips for giving a TOAST:
It is ok to write the toast and hold what you have written to refer to it.

Speak clearly and deliberately.

Maintain eye contact and smile.

Remember......it's not only what you say but the fact that you are saying anything in the first place that matters.

<u>Giving Opinions</u>

Just something a little helpful to remember:

Sometimes when people ask for our opinions, they don't really want them. It depends........they may just be actually looking for our praise or approval. Weigh it out before answering. If you can't say anything good then a good answer would be:
" I'm so pleased your happy"

Recipe on Table Manners

OH and by the way.......Table manners?
They still count. Keep some of the following ones in mind.

- If you are the recipient of a toast, do not sip your drink while the toast is being made, keep your glass up along with everyone else and be sure to be gracious by saying "Thank you" afterwords.
- If you wear lipstick, do not get it on your napkin.
- Keep your elbows off the table at all times.
- Do not put your purse, keys, sunglasses or cell phone on the table.
- Take food out of your mouth the way it went in. (if something went in your mouth that shouldn't have, remove it with the fork and dispose of it silently to the side of your plate)
- Leave your plate where it is when you are finished with your meal - don't push it away from you.
- Do not text under the table (if necessary excuse yourself to the ladies/mens room)

- Leave your napkin on the table if you excuse yourself. (Don't put it in the chair, yuk! That's nasty)
- When you are finished with your meal flip your fork upside down. The waiter should not have to ask if you are done.
- As always, do not talk with food in your mouth and do not chew with your mouth open.
- Do not talk on your cell phone at the table, excuse yourself and go outside. (only emergency calls are acceptable, otherwise you are sending the message that you don't enjoy the company of the people you are with so you are using your cell phone as an outlet to ignore your present company, it's pretty obvious).

RECIPE TO DO THINGS NOW

Twenty years from now you will be more disappointed by the things that you didn't do than by the ones you did do.
Keep that in mind and you will do things now.
Capishe?

RECIPE TO LOVE YOUR PARENTS NOW!
LIKE I ALWAYS SAY:
WE DON'T KNOW OUR TOMORROWS.
(we don't even know if tomorrow will come)
Tomorrow is not Promised
CAPISHE?

A Thought on losing my Dad.........

The things I miss sooo much...........
His sense of humor..........
The sound of his laughter.........
His strong opinions..........
His knowledge............
His mannerisms.........
How he formed his words..........
And most of all, his reliable daily caring phone calls.........
And most of all too (LOL) ....his voice

The things I miss about my Mom:

Calling her and depending on her to truly be the person I knew that could always call and ask her anything and she would have an answer, she could recall a date, a memory, etc. Back in the day she never forgot anything. She is very much missed.

I miss calling her to make sure she was ok. It doesn't matter what the relationship was. The fact is; it is a missing relationship. Now all hope is gone that it could ever be any different, some of my tears are for what never was. The good thing is, I loved her no matter what and gave her my best loving kindness. Not to mention, she did her best with who she was. I will always be thankful that she taught me how to walk, talk, read, write and spell.
OH and clearly she potty trained me (LOL).....these are things I know without a doubt. I always say: "Never forget anything good".

Here's the bottom line, if your parents are still alive, let them love you which ever way they know how, and let them know how much you love them, you will never regret it and you just always want to do the best you can! LIKE I ALWAYS SAY: "It is Better".

Chill out with......... REFRESHING Drinks!

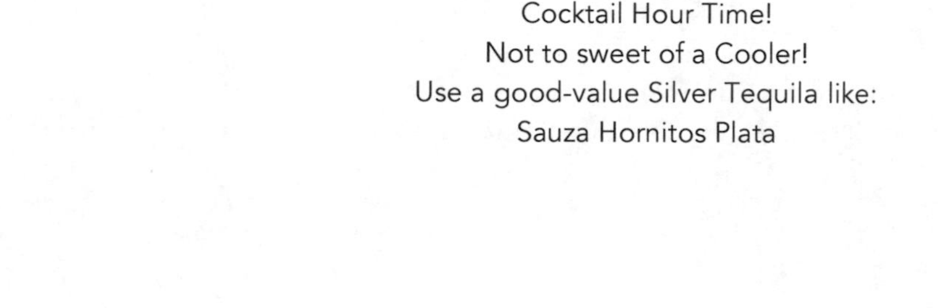

CUCUMBER TEQUILA-CITRUS-MINT FIZZ

This is great to serve guest – YOU will be a Hit!
Cocktail Hour Time!
Not to sweet of a Cooler!
Use a good-value Silver Tequila like:
Sauza Hornitos Plata

2 oz Cucumber Tequila chilled (recipe follows below)
1 Lemon wedge
1 Lime wedge
5 to 10 fresh Mint leaves
5 to 6 oz. Lemon-Lime soda, chilled

Fill 12-oz tumbler with ice.
Pour Tequila over Ice.
Squeeze Lemon and Lime wedges over ice; add to glass.

Put Mint leaves in one hand. Clap between hands several times to release oils; drop leave in glass.
Top with Soda. Stir gently.

1 Serving

ENJOY!

Cucumber Tequila

1 750-mi bottle Silver Tequila
½ thinly sliced peeled cucumber

Pour Tequila into pitcher (save bottle); stir in Cucumber. Refrigerate overnight.
Using fine mesh strainer and funnel, strain Tequila back into bottle. Store in refrigerator up to 2 weeks.

ENJOY!

1-2-3 FRUIT PUNCH

1 Can (46 OZ) Fruit Juicy Red Hawaiian Punch, Chilled
3 cups cold tea
1 Can (6 oz) Frozen Lemonade concentrate
Lemon Slices (wash Lemon really really good before cutting)

Have a large pitcher or small punch bowl ready.
Combine all ingredients
Stir
Pour into 9 or 10 ice-filled glasses.
Garnish with Lemon Slices.

ENJOY!

Grown-Up Frozen Lemonade
10 minutes to make
30 minutes to chill
Coastal Kitchen

You can also try another citrus in this recipe, such as fresh lime zest and juice, or even lime - or citrus-flavored Vodka. (You may need a little extra sugar, because it isn't naturally as sweet as Limoncello Liqueur.

1/2 cup Sugar
1 Tablespoon Lemon Zest
3 cups Ice Cubes
1/2 cup fresh Lemon Juice
1/2 cup Limoncello Liqueur (optional)

Garnish: Lemon Slices

Combine sugar and 1/2 cup water in a small saucepan, and cook over medium heat, stirring often, 3 minutes or until sugar dissolves. Remove pan from heat; stir in lemon zest. Let cool to room temperature, about 30 minutes.

Strain mixture through a fine wire-mesh sieve into a blender, pressing solids with a wooden spoon to extract liquid. Discard solids.

Add ice cubes, lemon juice, and Limoncello, if desired, to blender and process until smooth and slushy.

Serve immediately. (makes 3 1/2 cups)

ENJOY!

Triple Chocolate Slush
15 minutes prep time
cool for 30 minutes

This chilly drink will require a spoon until melted enough to switch to a straw

Although there is a bit of ice cream in this recipe, the ice makes it lighter and less rich than a typical milkshake. To keep the syrup visible on the sides of the glass, put the glass in the freezer up to 30 minutes before adding the syrup.

1 cup Milk
1/3 cup Sugar
2 ounces semisweet Chocolate, chopped
2 tablespoons unsweetened Cocoa powder
1 cup Ice cubes
2 cups premium Vanilla ice Cream
Chocolate syrup
Whipped Cream
Shaved Chocolate

Combine milk and sugar in a small saucepan, and cook over medium heat, stirring often, 3 minutes or until sugar dissolves. Remove pan from heat, and add chocolate and cocoa powder. Let stand 5 minutes; whisk until smooth. Let cool to room temperature, about 30 minutes.

Combine ice cubes, milk mixture, and ice cream in a blender, and process until smooth and slushy. Pour chocolate syrup down the insides of 4 glasses; pour in iced chocolate.

Makes 4 cups

ENJOY!

Cucumber Watermelon Crush

Cucumber water is so refreshing! This is a jazzed up version that includes fresh melon and mint.

1 English Cucumber, peeled and cut into chunks
4 cups seedless Watermelon cubes
1/4 cup loosely packed fresh mint leaves
3 tablespoons Sugar
1 tablespoon Lime Juice
Pinch of Salt
2 cups ice cubes

Combine first 6 ingredients in a blender, and process until smooth. Strain mixture through a fine wire-mesh sieve placed over a bowl, pressing solids with a wooden spoon to extract liquid. Discard solids.

Combine ice cubes and watermelon mixture in a blend, and process until smooth and slushy.
Serve immediately.

Makes 3 1/2 cups.

ENJOY!

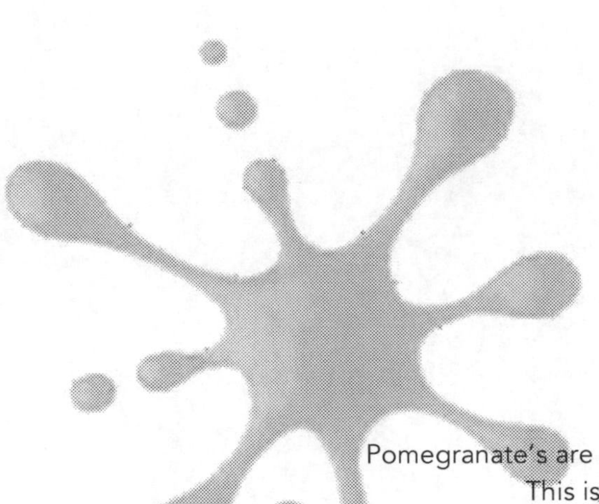

Pomegranate Mojitos

Pomegranate's are at their seasonal peak during the winter time.
This is a great drink at a Holiday Party!
Lime Wheels are the perfect choice for decorating the tray.
Makes 1 dozen drinks
Prep time 10 minutes
Chill 8 hours

4 cups Pomegranate juice
1 cup fresh Lime juice (from about 12 limes)
1 cup chilled Simple Syrup (1 cup water + 1 cup Sugar, see below)
2 cups fresh Mint Leaves
2 Limes, sliced
2 cups light rum
Ice
Chilled club soda

Pour pomegranate juice, lime juice, and simple syrup into a large pitcher. Stir in mint leaves, cover with plastic wrap, and refrigerate overnight.

Strain mixture through a fine-mesh sieve into a clean pitcher.

Decorate a tray with Lime slices. Stir rum into mint-infused pomegranate mixture. Fill 12 glasses with ice, and divide mojitos among the glasses, leaving enough room for a splash of club soda.
Finish with club soda, and serve.

Simple Syrup

In a medium saucepan combine 1 cup Sugar and 1 cup Water. Bring to a boil, stirring, until sugar has dissolved. Cool and transfer to a bottle; chill until ready to use.

ENJOY!

Are you a Juicer?

Check out some of these combinations, YUM!
These also go great with Granola & Yogurt!
You choose the amounts of each item according
to what you want to taste.

The Hierro: Spinach, Beets, Celery, Carrot Juice & Orange
The Vitalidad: Strawberry, Celery and some O.J.
The Calcio: Pineapple, Celery and O.J.
The Fancy: Cucumber, Celery and O.J.
The Dracula: Pineapple, Beets, Celery and O.J.
The Magic: Strawberry, Spinach, Celery and O.J.
The Vampire: Beets, Celery, Carrot, and O.J.
The Sulu: Cantaloupe, Guava, Coconut, Eggnog and Milk
The Bola Bola: Cantaloupe, Coconut, Eggnog and Milk
The Abracadabra: Avocado, Coconut, Eggnog and Milk
The Las Vegas: Spinach, Banana, Honey and O.J.
The Brazilia: Apple, Avocado, Coconut, Eggnog and Milk
The Malibu: Strawberry, Pineapple, Eggnog and Milk
The Palma: Coconut, Eggnog and Milk
The Oasis: Pineapple, Strawberry and O.J.
The Cancun: Papaya, Strawberry, Banana and O.J.
The Manzanillo; Strawberry, Pineapple, Banana and O.J.
The Bali: Pineapple, Spinach, Lime, O.J.
The Honolulu: Pineapple, Banana, Papaya, Lime and O.J.
The Fiji: Pineapple and O.J.
The Californian: Apple, Cantaloupe, Lime and O.J.
The Happy: Apple, Banana, Lemon and O.J.
The Sunrise: Pineapple, Strawberry, Spinach, Celery and O.J.
The Conga: 7 fruits of your choice and O.J.
The Acapulco: Cantaloupe, Guava, Coconut, Eggnog and Milk
The Wakiki: Pineapple, Banana, Coconut, Eggnog and Milk
The Healthy: Spinach, Lemon, Apple, Ginger, Celery, Lime and Cucumber.

ENJOY! ENJOY! ENJOY! ENJOY! ENJOY! ENJOY! ENJOY!

RECIPE FOR
Homemade Anti-inflammatory

Even amounts of the following:
Black Pepper
Turmeric
Garlic Salt

Here's another Anti-inflammatory Recipe:
Even amounts of: Fresh Squeezed Lemon Juice, Fresh Grated Ginger AND Creamy Honey, Mix together in a jar.
Take a tablespoon when needed
OR
Put 1 Tablespoon in hot water and drink as tea

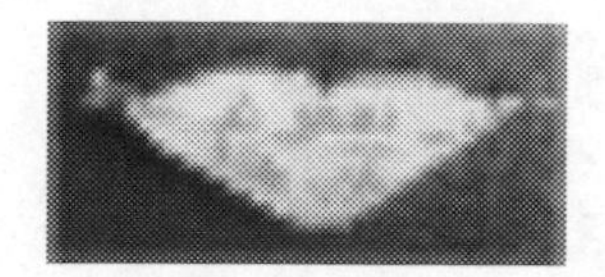

A Smile For You

Helping in the fight against Cancer

Thank you for your purchase of my book and by doing so you are supporting cancer research. I have had first hand knowledge of the effects and devastation of cancer through the loss of friends and family. I wish to continue the fight with your help through the sales of my book and this smile for you broach. I thank you from the bottom of my heart and hope that together we can make a difference.

Granny Nancy has partnered with other Authors in this fight. Lionel Douglass and his book, Feathers of Color Bigbird Live Book give back to the cause as well.
Purchase his book at Amazon.com & Barnes and Noble as well as Authorhouse.com

Thank You,

Granny Nancy

Don't forget to check out Granny's other web sites.....PeacefulMemoriesDvd.com

To purchase extra broaches for the cause, please send $5.00 each, plus $1.00 for Shipping and how many pins to: 92 Corporate Park #223, Irvine, CA 92606. Please complete the bottom of this page and send to the address below with a return self-addressed stamped envelope to 92 Corporate Park # 223 Irvine Ca, 92606 and receive a smile for life pin for your contribution against the fight with cancer.

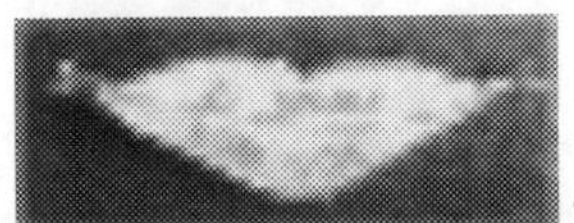
Smile for Life Broach

Send this portion of this page completed to the address above:

Name____

Address____

Phone#____

Email____

Love Granny Nancy's Kitchen
92 Corporate Park #223
Irvine Ca 92606